and interprets a client's experience. She demonstrates how the coach moves back and forth between the process of first eliciting and highlighting feelings and then helping the client thoughtfully reflect on these emotions. Kurt Lewin's famously said that there is nothing as practical as good theory. Students and practitioners of psychodynamic coaching will benefit greatly from this book; the former from the theoretical foundations this book provides and the latter by further honing their practice based on sound thinking. Read this book to make good on your goal of becoming a reflective practitioner."

– **Larry Hirschhorn, PhD, Principal, CFAR Inc., Philadelphia, USA**

"This comprehensive text is an invaluable resource for coaches and consultants, as well as students and clients of psychodynamic coaching. It begins with an overview of the history and theory of psychodynamic coaching which provides an understanding of its distinctiveness, especially in relation to human relationships. The remainder addresses the practice of coaching, giving guidance from beginning to end of the client relationship. Its emphasis on emotions and relationships supports enhanced adaptation to organisational challenges."

– **Professor Kathryn Haynes, Dean, Faculty of Business, Law and Politics, University of Hull, UK**

"'You believe to act purely rational – impossible!' With her new book on Psychodynamic Coaching, Dr. Claudia Nagel presents a highly valuable compendium to the subject of interpersonal and unconscious realities in organizational behaviour that senior managers and business leaders sometimes notoriously tend to either ignore in a pledge for 'plain rationality' or are rather convinced to master anyway. Claudia's work is firmly rooted in latest academic research, yet thoroughly inspired by her extensive practical experience in both, leadership roles in economics and global finance and psychoanalytical client work. Her work is masterful in her synthesis of addressing typical 'face value' situations in daily organizational life and tracing it down to the mental predispositions of humans and thus encouraging the reader to reflect on their own undercurrents of the unconscious. In doing so Claudia's work is remarkable for its very thoughtful human approach to the subject and the personality of the coachee. Her perspective embodies a great deal of respect and understanding for the individual, not least the subtleties of the coach–coachee–relationship. Great value for her and he who is willing to venture out beyond the trivial limits of the false belief in 'plain rational'. The reader will be rewarded by a fresh inspiration to reflect on inner motives, often non-related to the subject matter that requires decision making and so much more often than not distorting the outcome."

– **Heiner R. Bente, PhD, entrepreneur and supervisory board member, Germany**

"Life changes of individuals happen through guided deep reflections about the inner self and its interaction in different environments such as work or family. This book is more than 'just another' book about coaching. The 30 principles comprehensively describe what it takes to make lasting changes. Starting from theoretical backgrounds to the coaching process itself, it reflects the deep experience of the author in the field. Thus, *Psychodynamic Coaching* is not only recommended for coaches, but also for executives who deeply care for themselves and their teams."

– **Anke Dassler, Evonik**

Psychodynamic Coaching

In *Psychodynamic Coaching: Distinctive Features*, Claudia Nagel presents a comprehensive overview of the unique features of psychodynamic coaching. As leaders and managers acknowledge the need to understand themselves and their context by looking underneath the surface to improve their decision-making, psychodynamic approaches offer unique insight.

Psychodynamic Coaching: Distinctive Features covers not only the major theory but also the practice of coaching, giving guidance from beginning to end of the client relationship. Constructive, holistic and accessible, it demonstrates the impact and dynamics of the unconscious whilst illustrating the power of understanding human behaviour in the complexity of the modern world.

With a focus on emotions and relationships in supporting modern leaders adapting to organisational challenges, this book will be an invaluable tool for coaches of all backgrounds, academics and students of coaching and organisational behaviour, and also clinicians. It will also be a key resource for senior leaders for their own personal growth.

Claudia Nagel is a consultant, coach and senior advisor to international corporations and their board members. As an economist, organisational psychologist and chartered psychoanalyst, Claudia is an expert on leadership, strategic management and transformation processes. Deeply respectful of the human side of business, her background in finance and investment banking, and experience in different leadership roles, make her an invaluable resource for senior leaders.

Coaching Distinctive Features
Series Editor: Windy Dryden

Leading practitioners and theorists of coaching approaches write simply and briefly on what constitutes the main features of their particular approach. Each book highlights thirty main features, divided between theoretical and practical points. Written in a straightforward and accessible style, they can be understood by both those steeped in the coaching tradition and by those outside that tradition. The series editor is Windy Dryden.

Titles in the series:

For further information about this series, please visit
www.routledge.com/Coaching-Distinctive-Features/book-series/CDF

Psychodynamic Coaching

Distinctive Features

Claudia Nagel

Routledge
Taylor & Francis Group

LONDON AND NEW YORK

First published 2020
by Routledge
2 Park Square, Milton Park, Abingdon, Oxon OX14 4RN

and by Routledge
52 Vanderbilt Avenue, New York, NY 10017

Routledge is an imprint of the Taylor & Francis Group, an informa business

British Library Cataloguing-in-Publication Data
A catalogue record for this book is available from the British Library

Library of Congress Cataloging-in-Publication Data
A catalog record for this book has been requested

ISBN: 978-0-8153-9229-3 (hbk)
ISBN: 978-0-8153-9230-9 (pbk)
ISBN: 978-1-351-19963-6 (ebk)

Typeset in Times New Roman
by Apex CoVantage, LLC

To H.B.

Contents

Preface

Coaching in general shows a broad range of applications: it aims to support an individual's developmental process in job skills, career development, workplace performance, work-life-balance aspects, sports, physical wellbeing and also intimate relationships.

Psychodynamic coaching uses a very specific lens: it focusses on relationships and emotions in the work and organisational context of executives from "underneath the carpet". The aim of psychodynamic coaching is to help executives make sense of their inner-world, also called "the unconscious" to better deal with their individual and organisational context, since the unconscious influences the way we perceive the world we inhabit, how we experience ourselves and others in this world, and how we act, behave, feel and make decisions.

The contemporary approach to understanding the unconscious was initiated by Freud, Jung and other psychoanalysts at the beginning of the 20th century, but interpretation of the unconscious has a long tradition in poetry, literature, art, religion and traditional healing methods. Today's neuroscientific research underpins the former, seemingly intuitive and observational findings with studies on how different brain areas act, interact and react.

The need for coaching is growing in parallel with the decreased demand in administrative tasks and increased demand for emotional intelligence in leadership and individual development within organisations. With individuals having to dynamically and creatively adapt to a fast-paced environment with conflicting demands, emotional self-awareness and self-management as well as social relationship management have become key prerequisites for today's top managers. With growing digitisation, the capacity to provide a sense-making frame is also now expected of high-ranking executives. Psychodynamic coaching is the most suitable way to support executives in developing these capacities.

This book aims to provide an overview of the theoretical framework (Theory section) as well as lay the foundation for practical application of psychodynamic coaching (Practice section). It presents a guide for coaches, consultants and clients, and also a resource for academics and students who wish to understand this approach in depth.

As a coach, this book will help you to integrate aspects of the psychodynamic approach into your own coaching work and decide whether you wish to deepen your knowledge on the subject. If you are a coach already trained in psychodynamics, it will serve to refresh and update your knowledge. **As a client** you will learn how this approach works, how the process of coaching might look and how it supports you in improving your personal skills in a leadership environment. **As a consultant, academic or researcher** in consulting and coaching, social work or organisational behaviour and organisational development, you will develop an understanding of psychodynamics in coaching and consulting and the book will act as a guide to your students.

Part I of the **Theory section** introduces psychodynamic coaching, its history, aims and purpose. Part II explains and clarifies the basic theoretical concepts inherent in psychodynamic coaching and invites further theoretical exploration. Part III centres on the theory behind the application of these concepts. The **Practice section** is organised so as to follow the development of the relationship between the coach and client and serves as a guide to the coaching process from beginning to end. Part I looks at the preparational phase, Part II at the coaching relationship itself, and Part III at the conclusion of the coaching relationship.

As a unifying golden thread I have chosen **"emotions, relationships and being related"**. These are the underlying features of the psychodynamic perspective, because, as "social animals", relationships are crucial to our emotional wellbeing and our personal success: with oneself to manage emotions; professionally with colleagues, clients, suppliers and other stakeholders; and of course also in private life.

The psychodynamic approach is no easy-to-apply coaching method; it can be extremely helpful yet can also be risky for clients – working with emotions and the mind, especially with the unconscious, is demanding, and, in the hands of an untrained coach or an ill-intentioned individual, opening the mind's "Pandora's Box" can have detrimental consequences. Thus, sound theoretical and practical training is vital. This book shall serve as a **manual to this training**.

BASIC THEORY

The roots of psychodynamic coaching in psychoanalytic traditions

The psychodynamic approach to coaching incorporates an array of psychoanalytical insights, techniques and interventions focussing on the unconscious and its influences on human behaviour. As its name implies, psychodynamic coaching has two components – first, it places the approach in a psychodynamic context, and second, it clarifies the grounds upon which psychodynamic thinking and techniques are applied.

Coaching in the workplace has over the last forty years evolved into a valid means of developing people within organisations, particularly those in leadership and expert roles, to improve the performance of both the individual and the organisation. Coaching here refers to experiential consultation to individuals and teams in the work domain that focusses on the human aspect by helping the client to develop soft and partly also hard skills whilst learning without teaching them. Coaching concentrates on the executive functions (Roberts & Jarrett, 2006, S. 9), which are to conceive and manage multiple tasks in an interrelational context to achieve the objectives of the organisation.

The psychodynamic approach incorporates various psychoanalytic and psychodynamic aspects, concepts and schools of thought that have developed over the 125 years since Freud began to work on the unconscious. Psychodynamic theory is deeply rooted in psychoanalytic thinking, exploring the role of the unconscious in human behaviour. The unconscious can be best described as what lies "underneath the carpet" – unspoken, unthought, denied, repressed, forgotten, fantasised and dreamt, which influences our motifs, choices and behaviours – in short: the inner-world of the human being.

The dynamic aspect of the term of psychodynamics refers to processes that take place between different psychic instances (e.g. Superego, Ego, Id). The term has evolved from its original association with an **intrapsychic conflict** to being linked with the **relationship aspect** towards the middle of the 20th century. Today, relationships and emotions remain at the centre of contemporary psychodynamic theory and practice.

A short historical overview of the roots of psychoanalytic thought[1]

Freud's (1911) drive theory proposed that **neurotic conflict** lay between two different emotions or between an instinctual wish and a moral imperative, causing psychopathological reactions. Later, within his structural model, he developed the idea of conflicts and dynamics between the three instances of the mind: the Ego, the Id and the Superego (Freud, 1923). Conflicts can also develop out of dialectical tensions human beings are born into, particularly the fundamental human tension of autonomy versus attachment (Mentzos, 2009) (see Chapter 7). The choice of which to adhere to in a specific situation creates conflict and thus anxiety, yet at the same time fosters individual personality development. This consequently leads to renewal, dynamics, differentiation and progress, which C.G. Jung coined the *individuation process*. Jung founded his own school of analytical psychology, developing the notion of complexes, archetypes and the Self. Conflict here can appear within or between complexes on an intra- and inter-individual level and give rise to neurosis that may be addressed with the support of the transcendent function (Jung, 1959).

The development of psychodynamics then embraced the ego psychology first developed by Freud's daughter, Anna Freud, who contributed the theory of ego defences dealing with inner-conflict and warding off the resulting anxiety (Freud, 1936). In conflict-based psychodynamic theory, anxiety and fear resulting from or underlying conflicting choices are considered as the main driver of unconscious reaction. This is recognised as one of the major strands in psychoanalytic theory building and psychotherapy (Mentzos, 2009).

Around the same time, **relations** came into play with **Melanie Klein (1882–1960)**, the first child psychoanalyst of the **object-relations school**. She understood the *phantasised* mother-child relationship as central to personality development. In contrast, **Winnicott (1896–1971)**, the founder of the British object relation school, focussed on the *real* mother-child relationship and introduced the term "good enough mother" (1954), referring to the concept of the transitional object and the **transitional space** at the beginning of life. This is the intermediary space between mother and child, where they meet on a conscious and unconscious level and the child tries and tests fantasy and reality. The transitional object serves as a bridge between inner- and outer-reality. Later in adult life this transitional space develops into the basis for play and creativity.

Based on infant research, **Bowlby (1907–1990)** together with **Mary Ainsworth (1913–1999)** pioneered **attachment theory**. Ainsworth's focus was the infant's need for a safe base for developing secure attachment. Bowlby defined attachment more broadly as "the capacity to make intimate emotional bonds between people" (Bowlby, 1998), an innate psycho-biological drive to seek proximity with a familiar person (caregiver in infancy) when under threat. He also developed the notion of **internal working models**: basic models for relating with attachment figures that a child forms over time and which consequently influence all social relationships.

Bion (1897–1979) also significantly influenced psychodynamic theory with his model of the mother-child relationship, which presents the **mother as the container** and the child the contained. This theory suggests that unbearable states of mind are digested and psychically fed back to the child – the child perceives them and experiences them as a first form of thought (1962).

Bion is also of special interest in the work-oriented coaching context, as he has developed theoretical concepts around group dynamics and unconscious processes in working groups.

Contemporary psychodynamics is also informed by neuroscience, particularly neuropsychoanalysis. One of the founding fathers is **Mark Solms** building on the work of Peter Fonagy, Jaap Panksepp and Oliver Turnbull. One aim of psychodynamic neuroscience is to ascribe to mental processes an ontological status that is as real as that of neural processes. Neuroscience shares a fundamental aspiration with Freudian metapsychology, that is, to generate an accurate, large-scale model of the mind (Fotopoulou, 2012).

In summary, psychodynamic coaching focusses on the inner-world of the client in the context of leadership roles within organisations. It strives to **connect the inner- and outer-worlds** so that the outer-world, with its relationships and institutions, can be seen realistically by understanding and modifying individually influencing biases, blind spots, distortions and emotional reactions. The purpose is personal growth and development, to be in touch with one's own feelings and to become more emotionally intelligent. The approach works on the capacity to reflect on one's own emotions and the reactions and relationships that lead to them, to assess their role in the present situation and determine how to best handle them.

This work requires a systems perspective also – since the outer organisational world is continuously influencing the individual and their perceptions and behaviours. Psychodynamic coaching, hence, is often referred to as systems-psychodynamic coaching (Brunning, 2006) using the Person–Role–System model to investigate the relations, boundaries and influences between these three spheres from a psychodynamic perspective.

Although psychodynamics in coaching is rooted in psychoanalytical thinking, it is not to be misunderstood as psychotherapy. It is a psychologically informed developmental process, not a treatment for psychopathologies or emotional disturbances.

Note

1 In this overview I use some technical terms which I will explain in more detail later in their specific theoretical and practical context.

Psychodynamic coaching is not psychotherapy

Many psychodynamic coaches have clinical training, therefore it is pertinent to differentiate psychodynamic coaching from psychotherapy due to prejudices of confounding it with psychotherapy and psychoanalysis.

There is, however, a **significant overlap** between the disciplines. Both deal with behaviour, emotion and cognition, and seek to identify blind spots, defensive reactions, distorted thinking and irrational behaviours (Kets de Vries, 2006). Furthermore, both have a shared focus on uncovering unconscious and pre-conscious thinking and feeling and the application of concepts such as transference and countertransference (Beck, 2012).

The **major difference** between psychotherapy and psychodynamic coaching however lies in the fact that the latter is not a treatment for mental disorder or disturbance (Peltier, 2010). The handling of severe mental health problems or drug abuse is beyond the scope of psychodynamic coaching. Individuals experiencing such issues should be referred to a psychotherapist or psychiatrist.

A capacity for self-management is a clear prerequisite for a client of coaching, this is rarely the case in psychotherapy, where the development of self-reflection is an important goal; the focus of attention is on individual performance in the professional role in the work domain. Typical coaching clients are those in management positions that possess a good degree of job-functionality and performance. Coaching is goal and action oriented and focusses on personal growth and skills development. This includes working openly and actively with interpretations, hypotheses and projections. In contrast, the aim of psychotherapy is to reduce painful or pathological symptoms and work on neurotic or psychopathologic aspects of the personality. The psychotherapy process may therefore take considerable time and necessitate frequent meetings, whereas coaching is seen as a short- or mid-term intervention. With psychotherapy, responsibility for the process remains in the hands of the psychotherapist and is enacted through a hierarchical relationship and a more passive and reflective interaction style between the therapist and the patient. With psycho-dynamic coaching, a hierarchical situation is to be avoided; the coach functions as sparring partner, mirror and sometimes as an advisor, allowing the client to retain ownership of the problem and the solution; interaction is in general more active. Setting is another distinguishing factor. Whereas the psychotherapy session always takes place on the premises of the therapist, psychodynamic coaching can be conducted via email, phone or Skype conversations, or face-to-face meetings almost anywhere, and may include observational periods within the client's work environment (Kets de Vries, 2006).

Debate has arisen as to whether it is necessary for psychodynamic coaches to investigate early childhood experiences as a means of developing an understanding of the behavioural patterns of the cli-ent. In practice many coaches do integrate early episodes, whereas Vansina (2008) argues for integration of the client's recent past and actual inner-world only. Sandler (2011) is more open to this idea yet adds that there is no need for an in-depth exploration of personal his-tory, parental relationships and childhood experiences. My personal understanding is that whether or not to employ such an approach depends more on the particulars of the case rather than those of the textbook. In some cases, it proves extremely helpful to link dysfunc-tional behavioural patterns back to childhood experiences as a means of developing an understanding and awareness that enables behav-ioural change (see case example in Nagel, 2014); however, in other cases this approach may not provide additional insights.

Psychodynamic coaching can also be differentiated from technical guidance, which is more active and advisory; from career counsel-ling, which does not strive for understanding of emotional or rela-tional patterns; from mentoring, which mostly takes place between a senior manager and a junior staff member; and from supervision, which deals with consulting and counselling practitioners and their work with their clients (Schreyögg, 2010).

Basic elements of psychodynamic coaching

Having established what distinguishes psychodynamic coaching from psychotherapy, we will now turn to the five constituting elements of psychodynamic coaching.

First is the work with the unconscious which governs any psychodynamic approach:

- Much of human mental life is unconscious; it can produce behaviour that is incomprehensible or puzzling to the individual experiencing it
- Conscious and unconscious thoughts and feelings operate simultaneously and can be conflicting, necessitating compromised solutions
- Stable personality and social, mostly unconscious, behaviour patterns are formed in childhood and can persist to significantly impact relationships in adulthood
- Stable internal mental representations of the self are formed gradually throughout childhood and adolescence. These representations, which are often unconscious, guide social relationships and may provoke psychic symptoms
- Personality development entails learning how to regulate emotions, thoughts and social relationships, and progression from an immature, dependent and unconscious state in childhood to an ideal of a mature and independent state in adulthood.

(Kilburg, 2004)

Secondly, these key postulates require a specific **guiding attitude of the coach**, whereby s/he is the facilitator or midwife for the client's personal and professional development, not a problem-solver, advisor or consultant in technical terms. Although some define coaching as a subset of process consultation (Huffington, 2006), most consultants would define their role as being more active in contributing expert knowledge to solutions. What seems more appropriate for a coach is a facilitating and supportive attitude that encompasses meta-communication, whereby the coach supports the inner developmental process of the client by asking questions which engender a deeper self-reflection and foster insights into their own and others' unconscious processes and emotional influences, culminating in behavioural changes. The coach might also provide carefully considered feedback on the client's present reactions as a means of exploring behavioural, emotional and thought pattern recognition – without imposing their own view. The coach must strike a balance between maintaining a supportive attitude and judicious use of challenging questions without distressing the client. With this attitude of facilitation, the coach can establish a safe holding environment, and through the development of a trust relationship, the client will feel comfortable enough to open up and share their inner-world with the coach.

The **third** major element in the work of the psychodynamic coach is the client's process of **becoming more and more conscious** of her/his personal inner-world and the inner- and outer-factors that influence it. The basic idea behind this goal of developing consciousness of the inner-world is that events, feelings, thoughts and behavioural patterns that are external to the client's conscious awareness influence their choices and actions (Kilburg, 2004). Becoming more conscious means developing awareness of what is taking place in one's own inner-world. This process entails seeing, feeling and understanding the inner governing factors which influence our daily thinking and feeling – affects, patterns, rules, hypotheses, conflicts – as well as seeing, feeling and understanding how external events such as relationships with other people and social occasions provoke specific reactions.

The **fourth** element of psychodynamic coaching is achieving better **performance through personal development and growth** in the work domain. The basis for connecting personal and organisational performance and growth is not, as was believed up until the 1980s, setting clearer goals and improving motivational approaches (although this assumption still exists today), it is the acknowledgement that hidden personal and institutional factors can stall and sabotage growth and advancement (Obholzer, 2006). Behind this lies the assumption that organisational success (which is a positive state or condition defined by, e.g. financial parameters, client happiness or any way the organisation defines success) depends on individual contributions achieved through a high level of personal performance based on personal behaviour. By observing individual performance at the workplace, one can understand the degree to which an individual helps an organisation to reach its goals (Campbell, 1983, after Motowildo, Borman, & Schmitt, 1997). Broadly speaking, personal performance depends on personal skills (see Chapter 4) and can be differentiated as either task performance (which is related with participating in producing the goods and services the organisation is selling) or context performance (which maintains the wider-ranging organisational, social and psychological environment in which the task is executed (Motowildo et al., 1997). The higher one ranks in an organisation, the greater the significance of contextual performance to the management role. Task performance seems to depend on cognitive capability, whereas contextual performance is closely tied to the capacity to effectively relate within the organisation and its network of stakeholders and within the specific role the person is supposed to assume (Motowildo et al., 1997); in summary, to become a more effective leader in managing emotions and relationships, culminating in the transformational leadership style. Personal development is the prerequisite for becoming a transformational leader who will contribute positively to an organisation's dynamic capabilities, which are understood to be the core factor in achieving strategic success and enterprise performance (Teece, 2007). This leadership style can be elucidated as:

- Actively including the individual's perspective by paying personal attention and treating team members as individuals
- Being charismatic, presenting a guiding vision and mission, and instilling pride and self-esteem in team members, which will in return bring the leader respect and trust

- Inspiring followers by communicating high (but achievable) expectations through the creative use of symbols and explaining important goals in simple words
- Providing intellectual stimulation by fostering intelligent, rational and careful problem-solving (Bass, 1990)
- Fostering a flexible mindset and creating more options for thinking and acting to develop individual dynamic capabilities

From the perspective of the client in the leadership role, the performance need could be summarised as, "coach me, so that I can handle my relationship with certain situations/feelings/bosses/new sales targets/women/men/work/myself/employees, etc." (Beck, 2012, p. 15).

The **fifth element** takes into account that an individual cannot perform a role without an organisational system and a context in which the person and the organisational system both act and interact. The **person–role–system**, originally created by Browick around 1976, was developed into the diagram shown in Figure 3.1.

This very basic model is used in a specific coaching and consulting approach known as Organisational Role Analysis (ORA; see, for example, Newton, Long, & Sievers, 2006). It assumes that

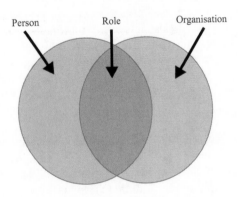

Figure 3.1 The Person–Role–Organisation Model

the professional role of the client is consciously and unconsciously shaped by the organisation as well as the individual. It focusses on the complex interplay and interrelatedness of the individual's psychodynamics and organisational psychosocial dynamics, which are acted upon at the interface of the two systems, represented by the professional role. Triest (1999) termed the key aspects of the professional role in the dynamic role concept the *informal* role – as the person perceives it – and the *formal* role – how it is defined by the organisation.

- The person's "circle" incorporates their life-story, personality, skills, competencies, talents and abilities, and also includes the personal context influencing the work domain, such as family relationships
- The role as an intermediary space can be characterised by the two role aspects, which are closely tied to the client's career ambitions, so far and for the future, as well as role ideas influenced by cultural and societal contexts
- The organisational level encompasses not only the actual working environment, but also organisational culture, structure and processes, not to forget the organisational context

(Brunning, 2006)

All these aspects consciously and unconsciously influence personal development and work performance, and in turn, organisational performance; therefore they are an integral part of psychodynamic coaching.

4

Reasons and occasions for psychodynamic coaching

The growing need for psychodynamic coaching results from escalating demands on leaders in response to the so-called "Fourth Industrial Revolution" and the "Second Machine Age" (Brynjolfsson & MacAfee, 2014). This is not just a matter of new business models, disruption of industries and the creation of new ecosystems, we must also envision that mind and machine will become more and more integrated through:

- Digitisation, big data and algorithms, the internet of (every)thing(s)
- Artificial intelligence, neuro-technological brain enhancement, robots, trans-humans (Bostrom, 2014)
- And the further application of new technologies that fuse the physical, digital and biological worlds

What effect will this change have on humanity in general, and specifically in the work domain? Jobs and professions will be refashioned, some will even disappear; the world will become more virtual, less tangible, less direct in personal communication. Obviously, this will influence the individual and collective psyche, yet we do not yet know how it will affect the mind and soul. It all depends on what we will define to be human and how we will deal with this humanness – e.g. emotions, empathy, fantasy, creativity, intuition, spirituality, problem-solving, self-consciousness and self-awareness, the ability to create art, literature, poetry, etc. – not to forget, with humans being social creatures, our deep need to relate to others.

Consequently, the underlying tone of our time is uncertainty, a feeling that leads to anxiety and fear (Nagel, 2017). Of course, executives also experience these feelings, and their exposed position necessitates that they deal even more with them. In times of constant change, leaders must find answers in order to direct themselves and their teams in overcoming these challenges. Although the future has of course always been uncertain, it seems as if, on all levels, technological enhancements have introduced an ambiance of limited accessibility. Hence, today's leaders must manage a basic dilemma – they are themselves unclear and uncertain about the future, yet they are facing expectations of demonstrating certainty, stability, trustworthiness and reliability to a no less uncertain workforce. The more uncertain the situations that demand assertiveness and clear decision-making, the more personal skills are required on a leadership level to contain and manage this ambivalence. At the same time, as we progress to an increasingly virtualised world, more and more employees will feel the need to reach for a sense of belonging, identity, purpose and recognition. This scenario implicates a very different leadership style, since in a less real and personally connected world, opportunities for exchange, building trust and giving recognition will likely be limited. Approaches to how we work will become more agile and more flexible, teams more diverse, hierarchies flattened and networking structures will take precedence. To meet these demands, it is essential that executives develop their personal skills.

By **personal skills** and competencies, we basically refer to the capacity to know and lead oneself and to apply this knowledge to relationships with others:

- Make more realistic judgements and reflect on emotional influences on decision-making
- Develop self-awareness and maintain a connection to emotions and the inner-world
- Reflect and manage emotions and develop behavioural strategies (Pooley, 2006; Huffington, 2006)
- Increase social awareness by developing empathy and by gaining insights into the conscious and unconscious functioning of organisational systems
- Manage relationships effectively – with oneself and with others

- Develop human resilience (Kilburg, 2004)
- Look for, develop and create a sense of meaning – for oneself and also for others
- Manage personal and organisational boundaries

Several of these abilities have been summarised by the term "emotional intelligence" (Goleman, 1995). Psychodynamic coaching therefore supports the development of personal skills and **drives and implements change** on an individual as well as organisational level.

Psychodynamic coaching can also support the process of understanding and developing **political thinking in organisations**, since the mechanisms of micro-politics are closely connected with the above-mentioned personal skills. **Strategic thinking** can also be improved, since considering an uncertain future stirs up emotions and activates all kinds of biases which can be more readily identified with advanced personal skills.

Psychodynamic coaching can also provide help and support in the following **special circumstances**:

- During transition from one role or job to another role or job, addressing succession questions (Peltier, 2010)
- At the occurrence of crisis, failure and traumatic events – at the individual as well as the organisational level
- Where a person has a "fatal flaw" (Kets de Vries, 2006, p. 255) that hinders career development (underperformance, abrasive behaviour, conflict avoidance, over-perfectionism, relationship difficulties, incomprehensible reactions)

To summarise, psychodynamic coaching proves effective when a senior leader wishes to further develop a connection with their inner-world and to grow personally and emotionally, and also when strong emotional states are encountered, when intra- or interpersonal tensions and conflicts cannot be solved, when at the individual, team or group level performance problems are prevalent or when dysfunctional behaviour occurs.

BASIC THEORETICAL CONCEPTS – RELATIONSHIP AS FOCUS

5

The unconscious as common ground – from soul to unconscious cognitions – a historical overview

Once closely tied to the notion of the soul, over the centuries the unconscious has lost its luminous character and mysterious connection with God, becoming secular and closer, if not synonymous with the psyche.

Since early history, human beings have held the belief of an existence in themselves of something larger than themselves – a something connected to a transcendent power such as a god that shall be appeased and positively influenced.

This something is in animistic societal structures understood as the **soul** to be imperceivably separate from the body and at the same time a mediator between the material and the spiritual worlds. Shamanic rituals were supposed to treat the illnesses of the soul; they were also used in Egyptian and Greek healing procedures, and later Catholic confession. These rituals are seen as the predecessors of psychoanalytic treatment (Ellenberger, 1970; Wulf, 2005).

The Ancient Greeks are said to be the first in the Western world to connect the notion of the **unconscious with soul**. Aristotle (384–322 B.C.) postulated soul (also psyche/anima) as the overarching (life) concept that held the essence of every living organism. In his model, the "greater soul" consisted of the "vegetative" (bodily), the "sensitive" (emotional) and the "rational" soul, of which the latter can be understood as mind, reason or nous. This first distinction between the overarching soul and the mind as part of it led to distinguish between psychology and philosophy, hence Aristotle is recognised as the founding father of psychology.

Over time this relationship between **mind and soul** grew more complicated. The idea of the **religious soul** was established by Augustinus (354–430), and focussed on faith, love and hope, underlining the soul's mediating role between God, truth and the material through its capacity for self-reflection and connection with the inner-world. Augustinus also introduced the idea of the **split between body and soul** in Western Christianity, an idea which still stands today and brought forth the question of where the mind is physically located.

Throughout the era of **Rationalism** the soul began to slowly lose its spiritual aspect. The notion of **the unconscious** came into play when Leibniz (1646–1716) attempted to integrate the idea of the inner-mind and the outer god. He used the terms "petites perception" and "unconscious and dark perceptions" as synonyms for the unconscious, which in "apperception" become conscious. These petites perceptions were regarded as a metaphysical vehicle similar to the immortal soul (Lütkehaus, 2005, p. 20).

Kant (1724–1804) built on the ideas of Leibniz to further focus on the **cognitive aspects of the unconscious**. Although Kant complemented the idea of the unconscious in that it also contained emotional and sexual aspects, he did not elaborate on this viewpoint. However, first ideas of traces of the childhood in the depth of the soul emerged, introduced by Johann Georg Sulzer (1720–1779) (Lütkehaus, 2005, p. 22).

In the following age of **Romanticism**, soul and unconscious were still not clearly distinguished, and the unconscious even regained its metaphysical nature. It was reconnected with the soul as the fundamental, irrational and creative ground for all consciousness (Pohl, 1999) and was consistently present **in the world of poetry and literature**. Schelling (1775–1854) used the notion of the unconscious explicitly in his work, describing it as the absolute and eternal foundation of the conscious, and compared it with the sun which cannot be seen by itself. During this period, Goethe and Schiller understood themselves as creative geniuses whose art was influenced by the unconscious, and Jean Paul (1763–1825) coined the term **"unknown inner Africa"** to denominate the unexplored unconscious (Otabe, 2013).

The 19th century brought about a more differentiated understanding of the unconscious. **Dynamic aspects of psychic processes** were introduced in Herbart's *Psychologie* (1816/1824), and Freud's teacher, Theodor Meynert, explained for the first time how perceptions can be suppressed and also suppress each other.

Later, through Eduard von Hartmann's (1842–1906) influential and bestselling work "Philosophy des Unbewussten" (Philosophy of the Unconscious, 1869/2017), **the unconscious** all the more became part of the **zeitgeist**, with Hartmann synthesising Hegel, Schelling and Schopenhauer and connecting the cognitive, irrational and volitive aspects of the unconscious.

Theodor Lipps's 1896 presentation at the third World Congress of Psychology, "Über den Begriff des Unbewussten in der Psychologie", was also of great influence. As part of this speech he stated, **"to renounce the unconscious in psychology means renouncing psychology"**. So, the notion of the unconscious had already travelled quite far when Freud, Jung and others began conceptualising psychoanalysis in the 20th century. Whyte (1978) summarises this journey:

> The idea of the unconscious mental processes was, in many of its aspects, conceivable around 1700, topical around 1800, and became effective around 1900, thanks to the imaginative efforts of a large number of individuals of varied interests in many lands.

What Lipps and others renounced, however, is the metaphysical base of the unconscious: "the unconscious is not hypothetical, not mystical . . . (it is) an expression of facts . . . and replaces the mystical forces and activities of the soul" (Lipps, 1896/1989, p. 246). **The soul had now finally lost its metaphysical connotation**, replaced by the psyche and the unconscious. Freud used the term "soul"/Seele often without any direct metaphysical connotations, interchangeably with psyche, making it the centre of his metapsychology. From his perspective, mythological conceptions of the world were projected on to the outside world. Thus, they can be traced back to the psychology of the unconscious, and therefore metaphysics should become metapsychology (Freud, 1901). However, the continuous translation of Freud's use of the German word "Seele"/soul as "mind" remains problematic, because it strips the word of its tradition and connections to literature, philosophy and religion, connections which Freud and his contemporaries were very much aware of (u.a. Bettelheim & Karlin, 1983) and even used in their theory building. In Freud's own words: "Psyche is a Greek word and is translated by the German 'Seele'" (Freud, 1905, p. 289).

So, for **Freud, the unconscious became the new metaphysics**; nonetheless, he attempted to overcome its mythical and religious foundations. At his 70th birthday celebration, Freud explained proudly that, although poets and philosophers had discovered the unconscious before him, it was he who developed the methods to examine it (MacIntyre, 1958).

In his well-known topic model, Freud differentiated between the pre-conscious, the unconscious and the conscious. The pre-conscious system – also known as the descriptive or latent unconscious (Freud, 1923) – is not part of actual consciousness, but can be accessed by it, and is attached to language by Wortvorstellungen (Freud, 1923). **The unconscious is the realm of suppressed memories and emotions, and also of socially unacceptable wishes, desires and ideas**. The suppressed drive never ceases to seek a full, primal satisfaction which is not achievable in contemporary society, therefore the individual is constantly subjected to a feeling of absence, a feeling of a paradise-lost which will ultimately be rediscovered in death (Rohde-Dachser, 2005).

In contrast with Freud, **C.G. Jung** maintained a connection with the ancient formulation of the soul and the idea of the unconscious as having both universal and individual components, as developed by Carus (1831–1846), which he translates into the **collective and the individual unconscious**. Jung's notion of the unconscious is less oriented towards suppression and non-acceptance, and more towards symbol creation that supports self-regulation of the psyche. In his model, conflict is not presented as the primary aspect, instead he underlines the importance of archetypes forming the base for individual complexes which develop out of personal experiences.

Lacan (1901–1981) advanced the perception of the unconscious as being structured as a language. Building on Lévi-Strauss's famous paper, "The Effectiveness of Symbols" (1949) Lacan developed a specific, although rather inaccessible language to describe his psychoanalytic insight.

In the middle of the 20th century, the **object-relationist perspective** (e.g. Melanie Klein), which, with early infant research developed into the "relational turn", transformed the perception of the unconscious from either a place in childhood, behind language, in the archaic inheritance, or within the brain, to a **presence in interaction**. This change resulted from insights into early childhood mirroring, attachment and the building of inner working models of relationships. Later in life, unconscious relational aspects surface in the interaction between two people in different ways, such as transference, countertransference and projective identification (see Chapter 8).

Neuropsychoanalysis and neuroscience introduced a very different, somewhat opposite interpretation of the meaning of consciousness and unconsciousness. The main puzzle facing the neuroscientist is not the unconscious mind, since even an unconscious mind can fully perform all cognitive operations of perception and control, but rather what consciousness is and what it is for (Dennet, 2017; Solms, 2015). In Solms's meta-neuropsychoanalytic terms unconsciousness is the "better", more effective state for brain and body (2015, p. 188 ff) since automated responses are a more efficient means of managing human interaction with the world. Consciousness (which is limited in the amount of information it can process simultaneously) arises only when needed: when something requires attention or focus, when the unexpected occurs and some kind of (re)action is necessary. Consciousness is therefore always linked with feelings towards events (threat/benefit to survival, pleasurable/unpleasurable) (Damasio, 2010), a link which enables the human being to assess and orient itself as to what action should be taken in a given situation.

The present consensus among the **cognitive sciences** is that mental processes can be conscious and unconscious. Unconscious mental processes imply that both perceptions and cognitions may occur without awareness. Earlier cognitive psychology understood **the unconscious as a wastebasket** (unattended or unrehearsed events), as a **filing cabinet** (passively storing memories which need to be actively retrieved), as **pre-attentive processing** (feature detection and pattern recognition as the basis for conscious attention and automaticity) or as **where cognitive and motoric skills become automatised** through extensive practice. All the above focus on unconscious mental processes, yet are at the same time based on conscious content.

More recently the idea developed that cognitions must be supplemented by **emotions and motivations**. Where cognitions are the mental representation of reality, emotions are the subjective experience of reality, and motivation is the guiding activation towards a goal (Kihlstrom, Tobias, Mulvaney, & Tobis, 2000).

When **emotional aspects** came into view, the **"affective neurosciences"** (e.g. Panksepp) emerged, and with them the idea of the emotional brain – that there is no thinking without feeling (leDoux, 1998; Damasio, 1999). In his influential work, Panksepp and his colleague Lucy Biven (2012) developed a system of **seven basic emotions** which follow a developmental path through life: SEEK, RAGE, FEAR, LUST, CARE, PANIC/GRIEF, PLAY. He uses capital letters to underline their very fundamental role. They are "instinctual emotional responses that generate raw affective feelings that Mother Nature built into our brains" and are also referred to as "primary process psychological experiences" (Panksepp & Biven, 2012, p. 9). These base feelings create an energetic form of consciousness full of affective intensity, which Panksepp refers to as "affective consciousness". They allow us to instinctively deal with the world and learn about its potential. Although one feels these affective states, one does not necessarily recognise that one is feeling them, meaning that they may be unconscious – an unreflective, unthinking primary process form of consciousness that precedes the cognitive understanding of the world and is experienced in an affective form. These primary emotional processes are "foundational pillars for the brain's mental apparatus" (Panksepp & Biven, 2012, pp. 13–16).

Historically, the study of cognitive neuroscience has excluded emotional factors; however, emotional and cognitive processes and contents can no longer be so clearly distinguished, with both now considered mental processes (e.g. Panksepp & Biven, 2012). Hence, affective neuroscience has become an aspect of cognitive neuroscience (Kihlstrom et al., 2000).

Kihlstrom (2013) summarises **unconscious processes** as manifesting in two different ways:

> First, some processes are unconscious in the strict sense that they are executed automatically, in response to certain stimulus conditions. At least in principle, automatic processes are unavailable to conscious introspection and are independent of conscious control. Second, some mental contents – percepts, memories, and the like – are unconscious in the sense that they are inaccessible to phenomenal awareness but nonetheless affect the person's ongoing experience, thought, and action.
>
> (p. 176)

Although there is no single definitive interpretation of the unconscious, and at present divergent theoretical schools allow for multiple understandings, there is a very basic consensus that feeling, thinking and acting are influenced by factors that lay beyond our conscious understanding of the world.

6

Personal development, personality and character in psychodynamic coaching

Psychodynamic coaching works with the process of making conscious the content of the unconscious that can inhibit an appropriate relationship with today's reality. This is the central endeavour of psychodynamic coaching and is closely linked to performance aspects in different role settings – in organisations and in life itself. **Personal development** is nowadays understood to be the key ingredient for individual and organisational performance (see Chapter 3).

Human development is a broader term than personal development. Linked to personality and character, it entails some notion of quality and integrity, of ethics and a good heart. It addresses a deeper layer of our psychic system that humanity has always sought to connect with. However, character and personality are complex constructs which refer to basic individual aspects that can be biologically, historically and psychologically influenced, thus human development can be understood from different angles. Here we will look at it from the perspective of: 1) personality types and traits, 2) philosophical ideas of character development, 3) the nobleness of the heart and emotional intelligence and 4) individuation as a developmental process.

Personality types and traits

Some see **personality** as an inborn trait, and **character** as being developed over the course of a lifetime. For want of a practical means of understanding personality, measures incorporating questionnaires and tests have been developed to structure and frame the concept. They are often used in organisations for predicting success and a person's performance in a new role. For instance, the Big Five personality test identifies traits such as openness, conscientiousness, extraversion, adaptability and neuroticism to illustrate the personality type. While the Myers-Briggs Type Indicator (MBTI) questionnaire identifies 16 personality types based on C.G. Jung's typology (see Chapter 21), the DISC model operates with four types (dominant, initiating, steady, conscientious), which are similar in their effort to measure and explain personality. Different personality types are supposed to perform better or worse depending on the demands of a particular position.

A more psychodynamic approach to personality is attachment theory. This theory describes **four attachment styles** which influence every social relationship a person undertakes. These attachment styles originate from how the person as an infant related to their caregiver, and are categorised as secure, ambivalent attached, avoidant attached, or distressed and disorganised (Bowlby, 1988). Bartholomew and Horowitz (1991) adopted these styles to create a two-dimensional diagram using the ideas of "the model of the self" and "the model of the other", to show the positive and negative attachment styles (see Table 6.1).

Evidence suggests that all these different aspects of personality are resolute and cannot be easily reformed. They can be detected

Table 6.1 Model of adult attachment

	Model of self	
Model of other (Degree of openess for intimacy)	Secure attachment style — Comfortable with intimacy and autonomy	Preoccupied attachment style — Preoccupied with relationships
	Dismissing attachment style — Dismissing of intimacy, counter dependant	Fearful attachment style — Fearful of intimacy, socially avoidant

Degree of dependecy

Source: Adapted from Bartholomew & Horowitz (1991, p. 227)

through focussed testing and interviewing – a practice often put to use in an organisational setting. The three non-secure attachment styles impact the way a leader connects and deals with people; they can therefore explain the difficulties faced and provide reasons for failure. Although personality is very reluctant to change, it is often talked about in colloquial interactions and in organisational settings, yet the difficulty of such change is avoided and rarely acknowledged.

Character development might therefore be a better term to use. As Charles Read (1814–1884) put it: "We sow a thought and reap an act / We sow an act and reap a habit / We sow a habit and reap a character / We sow a character and reap a destiny". One could then say that character develops from actions and the decision to act. This perspective was already held by the Ancient Greeks, for whom the word *character* was defined as "the engrained/the imprinted" and was used as a stamp in branding livestock. In ancient Greece, the development of character was closely connected with the "doctrine of virtues" initiated by Plato claiming wisdom, courage, temperance and justice to be the main **virtues**. In contrast, Aristotle understood a good life based on eudaimonia or happiness, the **highest human virtue**, as a goal in itself. Every human being has a task or a function in life, hence happiness is excellence in this task or activity, where "excellent" means "in accordance with virtues". Virtues are achieved by practising good actions. Possessing and exercising virtue delivered the best life possible for a human being (see *Nicomachean Ethics*).

Taking a moment to reflect on this, we can see that developing a "good" character to achieve a life of happiness and fulfilment is a continuous task of performing good actions by reacting appropriately; this is closely connected with the idea of not acting out of strong emotion, unconscious biases or deviations which are inadequate and do not take reality into account. It also implies determination in what one does and how one reacts – making conscious and self-controlled decisions in accordance with the individual way of being. **Virtue is thus a state of character concerned with choice**. (Aristotle II.6).

Without claiming to be philosopher, the point I want to make here is twofold: first, acting virtuously in the Aristotelian sense could provide a helpful **compass** for private and organisational life and, secondly, character is not something permanent and immutable, it is rather the result of continuous reflection and decision-making with regard to how one reacts and behaves. Coaching can support this reflection process.

Nobleness of the heart and emotional intelligence

Until the 19th century, an important educational endeavour and the overarching developmental goal was the "nobleness of the heart". Closely connected with "good character", this was understood as a complement to intelligence and referred to the ability to react in an emotionally educated way. In today's language it would best correspond with "emotional intelligence" (Goleman, 1995, see also Chapter 4), although the old-fashioned wording more clearly represents a certain attitude of kindness, empathy, friendliness, moral education, dignity, elegance and the capacity to open up to another human being – an attitude which is developed and refined over the course of a lifetime, and which has been lost sight of – its re-integration could also be a goal for psychodynamic coaching.

Goleman and Boyatzis (2017) expanded on his concept of emotional intelligence and made it more accessible for managers by incorporating a leader performance perspective, introducing twelve aspects that a leader must develop to perform well in a work environment (see Table 6.2).

Individuation as a developmental process

Whereas this kind of emotional intelligence employs a more functional or operational approach to working with how the individual deals with the world and with other people, psychodynamic coaching can, in addition, aim also towards an **inward-oriented goal**. The full development of one's own innate potential is best described by the term **"individuation"**. Individuation is the process by which the

Table 6.2 Emotional intelligence domains and competencies for leaders

SELF-AWARENESS	SELF-MANAGEMENT		SOCIAL AWARENESS	RELATIONSHIP-MANAGEMENT
Emotional self-awareness	Emotional self-control		Empathy	Influence
	Adaptability			Coach and mentor
	Achievement orientation		Organisational awareness	Conflict management
	Positive Outlook			Team work
				Inspirational leadership

Source: Adapted from Goleman & Boyatzis (2017)

individual develops uniqueness and differentiates their personality – "Man has to become what he is meant to be" or, as Erich Fromm put it, "Man's main task in life is to give birth to himself, to become what he potentially is. The most important product of his effort is his own personality" (Fromm, 1947).

In Jungian terms, the core activity of the individuation process is the unfolding and development of the Self.

> As an empirical term, the Self defines the totality of all psychic phenomena in human beings. It expresses the oneness and wholeness of the total personality . . . it comprises that which can be experienced, and that which cannot be experienced, or cannot yet be experienced. . . . In as far as wholeness, which consists of both conscious and unconscious contents, is a postulate, it is essentially transcendent.
>
> (Jung, 1921, §891)

The transcendent function is key to the individuation process, as it links the one-sided conscious with the complementary unconscious through the use of symbols as a creative sense-making mechanism (see Chapter 11).

7

Human relationships and the role of emotions and conflict in professional life

Emotions and conflict not only play a key role in day-to-day life, but also within the context of management, where they are mutually influential. **Emotions** can arise as a reaction to specific management situations, such as relationships with colleagues, subordinates, clients and other stakeholders, and also emerge from the individual inner-world. **Conflict** too can derive from relationships in the outer-world and within the inner-world, and catalyse emotions which then influence one's thinking and acting. Negative emotions and uncomfortable conflicts play a key role in psychodynamic coaching, since the limiting factors inherent in these mental states hinder personal, organisational and economic development and performance. Positive emotions can also be problematic since they too contribute to biases in decision-making, but we will focus here on negative emotions and the associated conflict situations.

Fear and anxiety

In a management context, uncertainty and ambiguity are fundamental features of many decision-making situations, since individuals in a management position cannot know or anticipate how the competition will act; which new, unknown or not yet fully known possibilities to seize; how heterogeneous possibilities shall be compared so a decision can be made and finally whether or not the chosen path will be successful (Bingham & Eisenhardt, 2011; Nagel, 2014). A high level of uncertainty and ambiguity triggers two central reactions: **fear, and the desire for control** (Hüther, 2005; Gilbert, 2006). Fear[1] is generally triggered by perceived threat and induces actions such as attack or defence (fight), retreat (flight) or to feign death. A manageable gap between the learnt and the new generally leads to curiosity and a desire for exploration. Yet, when that gap grows beyond what is manageable, uncertainty about the future is perceived as a threat. Initial reactions are retreat and abandonment, which can subsequently lead to an even existential fear, loss of acting capability and loss of control (Holzkamp-Osterkamp, 1975). Fear can be mitigated through cognitive intrapsychic mechanisms, such as redirection of attention, re-interpretation and re-appraisal (Hartley & Phelps, 2012). Other conscious cognitive fear-reducing mechanisms include searching for, applying and verifying tried-and-tested solutions; reflection on the conscious, emotional level; and also the presence of a close friend or family member (Hüther, 2005). If the experienced fear and anxiety, independent of cause, is overwhelming, it will be handled unconsciously by psychic defence mechanisms (see Chapter 8).

Another influencing factor on the unconscious level is the individual's **basic anxiety reaction**. Riemann (1961) described four basic forms of anxiety (see Table 7.1). Although every individual may express their anxiety in all four ways, one type is generally dominant. Which of these types is most eminent depends on the individual character and early experiences with attachment figures. Riemann differentiates between the anxiety caused by the outer-world of objects and the inner-world and relationships. Second criteria is the preference for either autonomy or attachment.

For coaching it is more helpful to formulate these anxieties from a positive perspective by describing them as a specific goal orientation (change, flexibility, conservation, determination). The poles of autonomy and attachment represent a fundamental human dilemma that leads to inner-tension and conflict (see next paragraph).

Before moving on to psychodynamic conflict theory, we can summarise that inner- and outer-threats may cause anxiety and fear and their respective reactions.

Table 7.1 The four basic fears and the underlying personality types

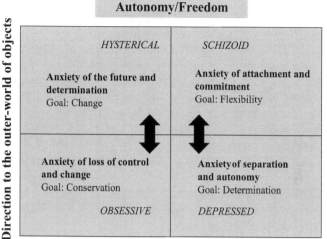

Source: Modification of Nagel (2017)

Conflicts

Conflict in the outward world may arise as a consequence of contrary choices that emerge in decision-making situations. This experience is routine for executives and therefore does not always lead to anxiety or fear. Yet, when the choices that arise become more existential because of their strategic nature and long-term implications, emotional involvement increases. Making the decision to concentrate limited resources on one technology, one target group, one production or one area can be painful, since doing so necessarily excludes an alternative. In management, the emotional pain of loss and the threat of taking the wrong path are consistently avoided and treated as a taboo subject – even though investigating the emotional anxiety or fear reaction here may reveal useful insight about alternative options.

Psychodynamic theory assumes **inner-conflicts** arise from the fundamental relational and dialectical tension between **autonomy and attachment**, which drives and motivates all individuals. Inner-conflicts represent the intrapsychic struggle between **self-related** tendencies of autonomy, independence, autarky and **object-related** tendencies and attachment, commitment, containment and solidarity. This inner-conflict leads to feelings of unpleasant inner-tension, because realising one side of the conflict would necessitate abandoning the other side, which itself results in the experience of danger and a subsequent feeling of anxiety. Schad et al. (2016) speak in this context of the "angst of tensions". In the individual intrapsychic world, anxiety shares its signalling function with external physical threats. Therefore, despite the outmoded Freudian assumption that anxiety is a basic drive, it is now common knowledge that anxiety represents one of the central axes of psychodynamics and psychopathology (Mentzos, 2009).

Normally, this basic human dilemma is continuously resolved, balanced and integrated over the course of a lifetime through a dynamic process. However, because of its threatening and painful nature, blockages or rigid, one-sided reactions may occur because the underlying fear cannot be managed and solved by the individual, and thus might lead to psychological disorder. Psychodynamic theory assumes that neurotic psychic disorders are based on unresolved conflict at a certain stage of psychic development linked with a specific fear. Therefore, behind every neurotic development lies a fear connected with a form of this basic dilemma or conflict (e.g. Mentzos, 2009). Neurotic reactions are based on psychic defences, which play a huge role in psychodynamic coaching (see Chapters 8 and 13).

Other reactions to fear- and anxiety-inducing threats are **cognitive biases**, which can result in unhelpful behaviours. These biases have been covered substantially in the management literature since Kahnemann and Tversky received the Nobel prize for their New Prospect theory, which explains why an assumed loss aversion can lead to seemingly irrational decision-making. A flood of biases has since been discovered. Here several are described and connected with the four anxiety types proposed by Riemann (see Chapter 7).

Table 7.2 Selected economically relevant cognitive biases and their psychodynamics

Topic	Type of bias	Description	Psychodynamics
Pattern-recognition biases: Sometimes patterns are suspected even if there are none	Confirmation bias	For an already developed hypothesis, an attempt is made to develop a confirmation rather than a rebuttal	Fear of change and an underlying fear of loss of control
	Salience bias	Recent or special events are usually overrated	Risk of false memory, trusting the nearby, and a fear of loss of control
Activity-oriented biases: One begins to act even though it may not be the best time to do so	Over-optimism	There is a tendency in the assessment of plans and results to overestimate the probability of positive results and to underestimate the probability of negative results	It seems more efficient to believe in winning than in losing; change is positive and needed => fear of determination/future
			Need for self and identity stabilisation, and an underlying fear of separation
	Over-confidence	Overestimating one's own abilities and expertise in comparison to others. One tends to take credit for success, but blames failure on the conditions	Need for self and identity stabilisation, and an underlying fear of separation

(Continued)

Table 7.2 (Continued)

Topic	Type of bias	Description	Psychodynamics
Stability biases: The current constellation will take precedence over an alternative	Status-quo bias	One prefers the current situation, especially when there is no pressure to change it	Fear of change and an underlying fear of loss of control
	Anchoring	In making an assessment, one tends to orient oneself to a previously determined value as a reference point	Fear of failure and an underlying fear of loss of control
	Loss aversion	The realisation of losses is largely avoided	Fear of failure and an underlying fear of loss of control
			Need for self and identity stabilisation and an underlying fear of separation
	Sunk cost	Irreversible costs are included in the decision-making process	Fear of failure and fear of change; an underlying fear of loss of control
Interest biases: Emotional preferences shape the decision	Group-think	One places emphasis on reaching a consensus instead of making a realistic assessment of the situation	Need for belonging, with an underlying fear of separation

Source: Adapted from Nagel (2014, pp. 67–68)

Recent research questions loss aversion's utility as a basic underlying psychological principle, implicating that negative events carry a larger weight than positive events and that this principle would hence show irrationality. It seems that modern studies cannot replicate Kahnemann and Tversky's results, which are the founding pillar of behavioural economics (Yechiam, 2018). Other researchers not only question the outcome or over-interpretation, but also claim the concept in itself to be fundamentally wrong (Peters & Gell-Mann, 2016; Taleb, 2018). These new research results will likely shed new light on the discussion of cognitive biases and seemingly irrational behaviours.

However, we can see how negative emotions such as fear and anxiety, resulting either from outer- or inner-threats and conflicts, influence and thus limit executives in their decision-making. There is a practical purpose to detecting biases as well as repressed negative emotions, since both are linked with defence mechanisms. Hence it would prove beneficial for executives to develop an understanding and awareness of these emotions and biases in order to restrict their influence in management.

Note

1 Fear and anxiety can be differentiated through the fact that fear is elicited by specific stimuli, is short lived and decreases once the threat has dissipated. Anxiety can also develop without specific physical danger and is understood as a state of sustained fear (Hartley & Phelps, 2012). In the context of this book the differentiation is not helpful, since uncertainty can be experienced as a feeling or can be caused by a certain environmental stimulus, and can therefore lead to both anxiety and fear.

8

Human relationships and basic working concepts

Transference, countertransference, attachment and defences

The previous feature briefly introduced the notion of defence mechanisms executed by the psychic system to protect itself against inner- and outer-threats, and the associated anxiety, pain or stress. These defences stem from three basic psychic processes:

- Projection or externalisation
- Splitting with the use of denial and suppression
- Introjection with cognate concepts of internalisation, identification and incorporation

These three processes form the basis of understanding the detailed workings of the defence mechanisms orchestrated by the psyche. They also underlie the phenomenon of transference and countertransference, the two major psychic tools the psychodynamic coach employs in diagnosis and intervention. The definition of these terms varies across the different psychoanalytical schools. They are presented here from a very fundamental perspective to provide a brief overview.

The Latin roots of the word **projection** serve well to describe its use in the area of psychology – "to cast a picture on to a surface". This is derived from the words "iacere", meaning "throwing", and "pro", meaning "forward, onto". The psychological application of the word indicates the act whereby one "throws" aspects of their own self on to another person or object. This act can take place under diverse personal involvement and to varying degrees of depth. For example:

- The individual transmits and thus "sees" aspects of an inner-object in an outer-object (e.g. the male boss is in his behaviour perceived as and confused with the father and the individual reacts to these aspects as if they were real)
- The individual can see itself as if it were the other (e.g. identifying with a character in a book)
- The individual sees and seizes the world from a very individual perspective which shapes their whole perception (e.g. professional deformation)
- The individual attributes denied aspects of itself to another person or object and deals with them as a straw man instead of acknowledging them as components of their own self (see Laplanche & Pontalis, 1972)

These different interpretations of projection share both the externalising of an inner-aspect and its identification in an outer-object, be it a person, a construct or a real thing. By inner-aspect, I refer to any representation of inner-life – an experience, a feeling, an attitude, a trait, a dream, a wish, a relationship, etc. Projections have a role in normal psychic reactions but can also emerge as a defensive reaction. In a psychodynamic setting, the objective is to make these projections – when they are unconscious and have a destructive, defensive or maladaptive character – conscious, and to (re)-integrate their content into the conscious psychic system. A simple way of recognising that one is in "projection-mode" is when one becomes very irritated and angry with another person. One can then assume that one is projecting an unpleasant and unwanted aspect of oneself onto the other. Traits or behaviours of this other person may also invite this projection. Jung refers to this as a "hook" for the projection onto the other (Jung, 1916).

An important sub-category of projections that plays a crucial role in management is **projective identification**. This term was coined by Klein to describe a process by which the separated content projected onto another person is unconsciously accepted by this person, who then identifies with this inner-aspect that did not originate from themselves. This may sound peculiar, yet it is a common occurrence (it can also be actively effected with subtle or even explicit manipulation). For example, a feeling of grandiosity or the opposite feeling of guilt that an individual cannot perceive or recognise in themselves is separated and projected onto someone else. This target of projection then makes it their own, and as a consequence acquires this feeling of omnipotence or guilt.

Splitting plays a part in projection also, since aspects of the inner- or outer-reality are split off and relocated elsewhere. Yet the focus here is on the inability to maintain these aspects as part of a greater whole. Freud used the notion of splitting to describe a division between two un-integrated aspects which take turns in coming to the foreground through behaviour. In Klein's theory, caregivers (objects) always have a good and a bad side, but the infant is unable to unify these aspects and "splits" either the good or the bad side off, causing one aspect to be projected and/or denied. This can be understood as **horizontal splitting**, where one aspect – normally the more ego-dystonic – becomes unconscious while the other becomes conscious.

Vertical splitting is a more complex process where the two contradictory aspects or experiences are held in mind simultaneously. This plays a role in fetishism and perversion, where the state of mind is characterised by a concurrent and unconnected acceptance and denial of reality. Splitting is an expression of a lack of integration and is viewed in self-psychology (Kohut) as a disturbance of the self or a narcissistic disruption.

Denial and suppression work as defences and are closely linked to projection and splitting. Denial is the refusal to accept reality or an aspect of reality, whereas suppression is understood as a holding off or keeping away the unpleasant aspects.

The concept of **introjection**, first developed by Sandor Ferenzci and later used by Freud, can be understood as complementary to projection. In simple terms, "good" things are (mostly) introjected, which means they are assimilated as an aspect of the self, and "bad" things are projected to the outside world. In Klein's work, introjection is the internalising of object-relations, which are primarily an individual's relationship experiences with early caregivers. Identification, internalising and incorporating are often used interchangeably, yet the first focusses on the personality as such and the latter on the physical aspect. Today, the term introjection has been superseded by "internal working models" (Bowlby, 1969). In attachment theory, internal working models represent stored unconscious cumulative relationship experience that controls our expectations and perceptions and creates a certain fundamental pattern that affects all future relationships. As a result, they control all emotionally involved relationships on an unconscious level.

Transference and countertransference can be considered a special case in regard to projection. Freud discovered that the analyst is often the surface for the client's projections of childhood relationship experiences. These experiences are re-enacted in the relationship with the analyst, whereby feelings connected with a past caregiver are reproduced as if the analyst were the former caregiver. This phenomenon occurs in day-to-day relationships and can lead to misunderstanding and relationship difficulties. In therapeutic or coaching settings, the unconscious conflict becomes accessible and interpretable, thus allowing the possibility of integration (Freud, 1912b). Transference can have both positive and negative dimensions. In the coaching or therapeutic relationship, an initial positive transference is necessary to create a trusting working relationship (Roth & Ryba, 2016).

Countertransference is what takes place on the opposite side of the dyadic client-coach system: the coach, analyst or therapist also has unconscious reactions towards the transference which induce specific emotional reactions. This can be seen as a repercussion of the emotional situation of the client. When these emotional reactions deviate from what the coach considers normal for themselves, the coach then knows that he/she is reacting on an unconscious level to unconscious aspects of the client. Due to the effects of countertransference, psychodynamic training requires an investment of time to understand one's own patterns and defences. For the client, it is essential that the coach understands from which aspect of his/her personality he/she is acting and does not get involved in unconscious collusions.

The basic mechanisms described here are the foundation of psychodynamic work. Most of the assumptions, insights or ideas the coach develops stem from observing defensive reactions of the client or the psychic system. In-depth knowledge and understanding of these mechanisms and their combinations in practical reality is essential when working with clients (see also Chapter 13).

9

Neuroscientific foundations of human relationships

New insights for psychodynamic coaching

Neuroscience has gained increasing traction in the field of psychology and psychodynamic theory. Through an understanding of how and where emotions develop and how they are connected with thought, the basic influencing factors of (mal)adaptive behaviour can be better known and governed.

Panksepp and Biven (2012) identified seven fundamental emotional characteristics (basic emotions) (see Chapter 5):

- SEEKING resources
- RAGE to protect resources (unpleasant)
- FEAR as a defence
- LUST controlling sexuality (a social response, strongly connected to seeking)
- CARE as maternal and nurturing behaviour (reward)
- PANIC due to separation distress
- PLAY as social engagement (reward)

These affective systems form the emotional basis of every human being and serve to make the individual aware of their needs and take corresponding action to meet them.

Building on Panksepp's work in affective neurosciences, Solms developed and applied a new approach to mind, brain, body and consciousness in the area of neuropsychoanalysis. Consciousness is generally understood to be located in the cortex, the large frontal region of the brain. Yet consciousness can only be observed from a subjective perspective; it is connected with mind; it is a mental process. The individual as a conscious being must, as Solms cites Nagel (1974), "*feel* like something to be that thing (e.g. that individual being)" (Solms, 2014, p. 50, italics in original). Neuroscience has long sought the neural correlates of consciousness; these are now understood to be affects, the basic quality of consciousness (Panksepp, 1998). Only when one feels something can one recognise and be aware that one is conscious and alive. It is only through the "extending" of affect onto perceptual and mnemic representations that we are able to also feel them, and thereby have the relatively complex experience: "I feel like this about that" (p. 50). These affective feelings have a motivational impact; they make us do something (seek more, run away, etc.) because they indicate that certain needs are not being met (physiological needs such as food or psychological needs such as satisfying curiosity). When these affective feelings become conscious, they tell us that we must solve the problem and that we must take some sort of action. In response to this we attempt to develop a solution. If the needs are met, the solution is stored as cognition in the working memory of the brain; it becomes a representation. This is the first step of a learning process. When these cognitions/memory traces are repeatedly re-used, they gradually become automatised. Therefore, cognitions first develop into cognitive consciousness and later, when they are automatised, are consolidated and become unconscious. This means also that only through activated affect can memory traces become conscious with their representations – affect motivates and focusses attention.

Solms's approach is very similar to what Freud described as "cathexis" (Besetzung), where the affect connects with the memory trace (see Figure 9.1).

Various areas of the brain play a role in this learning process. Their function is to help ensure the needs of the individual are met. Here we refer to the non-declarative, implicit learning process, specifically associative learning connected with an emotional response involving the amygdala (see Figure 9.2).

Body <-> Mind

- Intrabody (internal sensors: eg not enough energy)
- Extrabody (perception of unpleasant experience)

Homeostasis (preferred state)

A need is not met (Problem: Inequilibrium)

brain reaction: activation system ->arousal

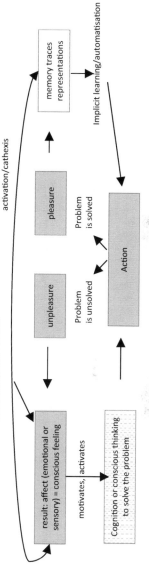

pleasure

unpleasure

Problem is solved

Problem is unsolved

Action

activation/cathexis

memory traces representations

Implicit learning/automatisation

result: affect (emotional or sensory) = conscious feeling

motivates, activates

Cognition or conscious thinking to solve the problem

Figure 9.1 Function of affects

Source: Author's own drawing

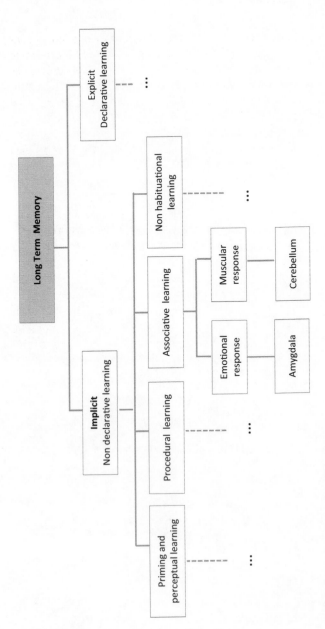

Figure 9.2 Long-term memory development

Source: Adapted from Solms (2017, p. 17)

Solms's (2013) conclusion is that the id is conscious (not unconscious as speculated by Freud), since affects must first become conscious to operate, whereas the ego is unconscious as it contains memory traces, which are largely unconscious and must be stimulated by an affect to become conscious. This representation, however, is part of the non-declarative system and cannot be brought back into consciousness; it is only the affect which is conscious.

This theory, when applied, will change the treatment of patients and of course the way coaching is delivered. It will become necessary to shift focus to the affect the person is experiencing and suffering from and also from behaviour and actual emotions to the affective system and the still unresolved problem. The learnt patterns of action – which are functioning as predictions of what will meet the given need – often do not work and cause the person to be unhappy. Panksepp's affective systems are an important guide to the inner-feeling structures in terms of understanding in which system the question or problem is located, and it is crucial for them to be understood and worked with. Countertransference, the transference of the feelings of the other, in this perspective (as well as others) is key to developing an idea of where to start working. Ultimately, the client must learn to face up to unpleasant facts and develop new patterns of action accordingly (Solms, 2017).

10

The system as significant context

Psychodynamic coaching is more than simply the interaction of two people; the context influences the process also. We have already assumed that the client is seeking support in their professional role, so the context is primarily shaped by the generally dominant system, the organisation. Yet the client is also part of smaller systems such as their family or friend groups, and larger systems such as society or a nation. There are two main ways in which systems can play a part in the coaching process: they can either act as the influencing context for the client, which is represented as an internal object, or as the outer-reality context that is influenced by the client.

The **systemic approach** views the individual as a nexus of relationships rather than being bound by their own skin (Reed & Bazalgette, 2006). This perspective is important because "the emotional world of organisation can appear simply as a function, a kind of artefact, of human relations within" (Armstrong, 2006a, p. 93), which suggests that these relationships do influence the individual inner emotional world.

The development of a **systems-psychodynamic** school of thought was initiated by the Tavistock Institute and first systematised by Miller and Rice (1967). Here, system refers to a perspective which frames the experience of the working person – the structural aspects such as organisational design, levels of authority, division of labour and reporting relationships, as well as the organisation's tasks, the nature of the work task, processes, activities, the mission, the primary task and the primary risk. The resulting group and social processes can be a source and a consequence of unresolved or unrecognised organisational and individual difficulties (Gould, Stapley, & Stein, 2001). The systems-psychodynamic perspective thus implies working simultaneously from the inside-out and the outside-in without preference for either approach (Armstrong, 2006a). The focus of systems-psychodynamic coaching is the person-in-role and the accompanying context that consists of multilayered organisational and social fields (Brunning, 2006).

The Tavistock Method established the foundations for systems-psychodynamic coaching. Following World War II, in the late 1940s, Bion, a trained Kleinian psychoanalyst, conducted a series of small study groups at London's Tavistock Institute of Human Relations, later published as "Experiences in Groups". These studies brought the work group as a collective entity into focus, not only regarding the roles of the individual, but also the dynamics of authority, leadership relations and boundaries. At the same time, the systems theory perspective was introduced into organisational and social psychology (e.g. Buckley, 1967; Katz & Kahn, 1966) and economics (where the focus remained on the individual: Simon, 1947, 1957; March & Simon, 1958; Cyert & March, 1963). Rice (The A.K. Rice Institute in the US is the equivalent of the Tavistock Institute in Great Britain) developed the view that individuals cannot be separated from the context of the groups in which they participate, a view which shaped the contours of the group-relations conference as a teaching modality. Under Rice's influence, group work in the 1960s in Great Britain focussed on group relations.

Groups can develop from a conscious choice to perform a task, which is the basis for organisational work. They can also develop as a response to emotional threat. The group behaves as a system and can be understood as a whole. The **"group-as-a whole"** approach was mainly developed by Michael Foulkes and Kurt Lewin (Ettin, Cohen, & Fidler, 1997):

- The primary task of any group is to do what it must to survive
- The group has a life of its own only as a consequence of the fantasies and projections of its members
- The group uses its members in service of its primary task
- The behaviour of a group member is the expression of his or her own needs, history and behavioural patterns, and the needs, history and behavioural patterns of the group

- Whatever the group is discussing or whatever task it is performing, it is always reflecting on itself
- Understanding the process of the group provides group members with heightened awareness and the ability to make previously unavailable choices about their identities and functions in a group setting

(Banet & Hayden, 1977)

Even when functioning as a work group pursuant to a clear organisational task, groups are prone to derail themselves and revert to a defensive basic assumption mode (Ettin et al., 1997) (see Chapter 14). With regard to the coaching process, the group as a system approach serves two purposes: it helps with understanding the influences of the group context on the individual, since the group shapes the roles, relationships and identities of its members (Bion, 1962), and can also be used for a psychodynamic team-coaching approach.

The organisation as a system, in regard to its purpose, can be characterised by two basic governing conceptions: the primary task, and the primary risk. The **primary task** is that which the system, group or company has been established to fulfil. The **primary risk** is that which is inherent in introducing a new way of doing things or going in a new direction (Hirschhorn, 1999). The necessity of choosing a different task, or a task at all creates emotional reactions such as anxiety in both leaders and followers. This anxiety is often not expressed consciously but remains unconscious and impedes decision-making. Oscillating ambivalently between two alternative primary task strategies is therefore a possible reaction.

The individual looking at the system

There are two ways in which the organisation as a system can be present in the discourse between the client and the coach: as internal reality and an object in the mind, or as external reality independent of the client and coach. The internal reality, the **"object in the mind"**, is

> not the client's mental construction of the organisation, but rather the emotional reality of the reality that is registered in him or her, that is infecting him or her, that can be owned and disowned, displaced or projected, denied, that can also be known or unthought.
>
> (Armstrong, 2006b, p. 52)

When considering the organisational object, the question of whether an organisation has an emotional life of its own arises. Armstrong argues that the organisational object as a point of origin of psychic experience can be defined by its boundary conditions such as enterprise, process, structure and the context within which it is embedded (Armstrong, 2006a), that generate the emotional patterning within. Therefore, the individual inner-reality can be interpreted to aid in understanding the individual's own emotional patterns and why they emerge in the organisational setting. This can also provide insight into the organisation as a whole, the nature of the primary task, how it is structured and the challenges and dilemmas it faces (Armstrong, 2006a). In this way, the inner-reality of the individual is connected with the outer-reality of the organisation, which can thus be understood and subject to intervention.

The link between the organisation-in-the-mind and the **outer-reality** lies in the individual's role. The role can be understood as the place, the area or the interface between personal and social systems (see Chapter 3). Aspects of these roles can be differentiated into formal (defined by the organisation) and informal (including conscious and unconscious aspects of the individual) (Sievers & Beumer, 2006). The person is then the "person-in-role" and undergoes a process of finding, making and taking the role (Reed & Bazalgette, 2006). Organisational Role Analysis is the applied method of this role conception (see Chapters 3 and 20).

APPLICATION IN COACHING – USING THE RELATIONSHIP

11

Understanding the inner-landscape

Creating and transforming meaning

Meaning- or sense-making in therapy and coaching is one of the fundamental concepts of psychodynamics. It is a process whereby the coach becomes fully immersed in the client and their story. Bion (1970) talks of "eschewing or suspending memory, desire, understanding and sense impressions" (Vansina, 2008), which involves maintaining awareness of one's own personal emotional experiences whilst simultaneously listening, interpreting and choosing when and how to intervene. This multilayered process is complex, and appropriate training is required so as to avoid unconscious collusion with the client's unconscious demands. With this in mind, instead of the Freudian idea of free-floating attention, it seems more appropriate to apply "equally divided attention" (Bion, 1970) to the here and now, the emotional situation of the individual, the respective system, one's own personal experiences and potential interventions. This multilayered approach also entails that by coaching a client, both client and coach will change.

Meaning itself can have different meanings, there is no objective "reality" or "truth". We can talk about meaning attribution as a **social process**, where meanings of constructs and words change with the language game, time and culture. Meaning is always a social construction, there is no objective "reality" or "truth".

Meaning also arises from **personal attributions** to life events, experiences, thoughts and actions. Human beings continuously search for meaning and attempt to subjectively make sense of what they perceive in the inner- and outer-world. When a client presents how they are behaving in their role in the workplace, the objective of psychodynamic coaching is to enlarge their perspective and approach the situation from different angles. When a first attributed meaning is explored, it can have a knock-on effect of transforming the overall life-story.

Meaning can emerge, and this **emergence** can be cultivated through an attitude of not-knowing and negative capability. Negative capability is "the capacity to sustain reflective inaction" (Simpson, French, & Harvey, 2002, p. 1210). The origin of this notion goes back to Keats, who wrote, "a person is capable of being in uncertainties, mysteries, doubts, without any irritable reaching after fact & reason" (Keats, 1970, p. 43). This mechanism of emergence can also become a pro-active sense-making process "by which pieces of data are brought together into a congruent whole that draws new light and gives meaning to what may appear as unrelated. It often touches more an *invention* than a *discovery* of concealed meaning" (Vansina, 2008, p. 111, Hervorh im Org).

Meaning can therefore be made on **different levels**:

- The meaning of the situation the client is experiencing (what does the situation itself mean for the client? How can it be understood? What can be done with it?)
- The meaning of being in this particular situation (how did the client get into the situation, are there any existing patterns that may have led to this outcome?)
- Meaning for the system one is in (what does the situation convey about the system?)
- Meaning of the evolving life-story (how is the situation part of the overall life-story of the client and how does it change the narrative or the future?)

The brain continuously makes connections between past and present, between existing patterns and new experiences. A positive feeling of "a-ha" or "eureka" arises when new connections are created, which brings positive energy and opens up the mind to new possibilities.

In the consulting room, the development of meaning can be fostered using a number of techniques, such as 1) the coach employing an attitude of not-knowing and ignorance, 2) through a process of co-creation, 3) by working with symbols on every level they emerge and 4) by mentalising.

An **attitude of ignorance** on the part of the coach is key to unfolding new meaning. It creates a reflective space in which the client can be silent, ponder, express and explore their personal emotions and perspectives without inhibition or censorship. Interpretations are not given, but can be tested, accepted or discarded. The situation of being in silence together, which Lawrence (2006) understands as "rêverie", occurs also when coach and client are stuck and have no words – at this point the boundaries of the unconscious have been reached and mutual effort is required to remain in the presence of the unconscious so that together new meaning can be developed.

In this joint process, a curious mutual exploration of thoughts, ideas and feelings leads to the **co-creation** of meaning. Jung (1946) beautifully compares this with the bath in the Rosarium Philosophorum, in which the two bathers are transformed by the process of diving into the water representing the unconscious (Figure 11.1; see also Jung, 1935).

While a reflective space can be created by the coach and the client, the arising content must itself be understood so as to allow meaning to unfold and develop. According to Freud and Jung, the unconscious expresses itself through common channels such as dreams, fantasies and **symbols**, and archetypes that arise from such. Myths, fairytales and art can also be understood as expressions of the unconscious. Whereas Freud saw dreams as the "royal road" to the unconscious, Jung understood all symbols and images to be the language of the soul. Approaching the unconscious, which has no language as such, can be achieved by working with symbolic meaning.

In the process of coaching, symbols can emerge and can be interpreted on several levels (see Chapter 25). Working with symbols is working with the inexpressible, the unsayable, the unthinkable – images and symbols always convey more than the superficial and obvious content. It is this basis that makes symbols the ideal starting point from which to approach the unconscious, because there is always more than one layer to their meaning. When working with

Figure 11.1 The bath in the Rosarium as a symbol of a mutual transformation process

Source: Wiki commons

Credit: Wellcome Library, London. Wellcome Images images@wellcome.ac.uk http://wellcome images.org. Woodcut depicting the king and queen seated in a stone bath holding flowers and a dove hovering above.

symbols, a new meaning, a new third can arise – this is often connected with a moment of strong emotion (Roth, 2003; Jacobi, 1957).

The **capacity to symbolise** is closely connected with and builds on the capacity to mentalise. **Mentalising**, a concept developed by Peter Fonagy and his colleagues (Fonagy, Gergely, Jurist, & Target, 2002), refers to the ability to perceive mental states in oneself and others, and to implicitly and explicitly acknowledge that these mental states can represent reality from different angles (Allen, Fonagy, & Bateman, 2008). It is the capability of "holding mind in mind" or, "holding heart and mind in heart and mind", and how we make sense of our own and other people's thought processes and emotional states. It is about feeling, recognising feelings, and at the same time thinking about these feelings, and can be described as looking at yourself and others from the outside and the inside. Mentalising is a basic human ability. It differs from empathy in the sense that empathy involves feeling in parallel what the other feels and not only reflecting upon feelings.

The capacity to mentalise is a prerequisite to the creation of meaning and is also highly relevant to leadership. Self-awareness, self-reflection and emotional self-regulation as well as relationship creation between stakeholders are all based on this ability. Mentalising can be trained and improved and is best employed with a not-knowing attitude, incorporating wonder, curiosity, inquiry and a willingness to develop new perspectives.

Developing and understanding the symbolic aspects via not-knowing, exploring, mentalising and contemplating in the reflective space are the core ingredients of meaning creation in the coaching relationship. (see Chapter 25)

12

Dealing with different leadership types

Coaches encounter a diverse array of people in leadership scenarios, therefore it is useful for a coach to develop a theoretical understanding of different **leadership styles** based on personality structures, their characteristics, their risks and possible disorders. We must, however, be aware that labelling people does not do justice to the complexity of their personality. Oversimplifying can denigrate the individual and cause them to identify with the label and, as a consequence, lead to associated action, i.e. self-fulfilling prophecies.

Personality involves the essence of a person (see Chapter 6) and although the earliest formed psychological structures are difficult to change, they are not unalterable; they can be influenced, and develop throughout a lifetime. Personality structures vary from healthy and functional, to severely maladapted or mentally ill. Mentally healthy people do not distort reality, they can be attributed with a positive psychological and physical energy, an ability to engage with life, empathy, accurate self-awareness, integrity, day-to-day interaction skills, flexibility and humour (Peltier, 2010). Most clients will probably fall into this category or show minor deficiencies in some areas.

Kernberg (1998) proposes **five personality characteristics desirable for rational leadership** (compared to irrational in the sense of mentally unhealthy):

1 Intelligence
2 Honesty and incorruptibility
3 The capacity to develop and maintain intensive relationships with other people
4 Healthy narcissism
5 A healthy, justified and anticipatorily paranoid attitude, as opposed to naïveté

The wording of the latter two characteristics, healthy narcissism and paranoia, indicates the existence of unhealthy aspects of these characteristics also. The difference between a trait and a psychopathology is the extent of distress and disability caused (see *Diagnostic and Statistical Manual of Mental Disorders*, DSM). One can differentiate between mental disabilities such as schizophrenia, bipolar disorder and dementia, and psychopathologies such as anxiety, depression, ADHD (attention deficit/hyperactivity disorder) and personality disorders. An awareness of these personality pathologies is beneficial to the coach, because they have the potential to not only undermine, but destroy people and organisations.

The **four anxiety styles** (see Chapter 6) and the connected personality structures can be integrated into a leadership style framework. I reference these styles here because they connect with two major aspects of leadership life: they explain how a leader is prone to making decisions, and how a leader deals with paradoxes in general – both basic qualities of leaders that are continuously demanded and challenged by leadership situations.

From this perspective we can differentiate between the schizoid, depressive, hysteric and obsessive leadership type or style, which I will describe in their extremes for illustration purposes (see Riemann, 1961; Kernberg,1984 for the following descriptions).

Schizoid leaders can be found in large hierarchical organisations. They can be best described as isolated, distant and unavailable, and are characterised by a difficulty with establishing and maintaining human interaction. The schizoid decision-making style is isolated and suffers from a lack of integration of others' needs and opinions. These types produce excessive cautiousness and hypersensitivity in others and provide their followers with little emotional warmth or support.

Complementary in regard to the paradox of autonomy and attachment is the **depressive character**, which is rarely found in leadership positions. However, these types may seek coaching because they feel that their career is going nowhere or do not understand why they cannot advance. They can be described as overly adaptive, helpless and dependent, but often with unconscious aggressive impulses. The decision-making style associated with this type would be to integrate the needs and viewpoints of too many, and as a consequence face difficulty coming to any decision at all. Anxiety hinders the individuation process of the depressive character, because a commitment to seeing this process through would entail autonomy and independence, which could lead to fear of being alone, isolated and separate from the other.

The **obsessive character** focusses on orderliness, precision, clarity and control. These types can be found in statistic or number-oriented positions, e.g. finance or financial controlling.

The decision-making style of the obsessive character can lead to choices being made which do not allow space for change and room for the new. This style fosters stable delegation of authority and clarity, and thus functions rather efficiently from an organisational viewpoint (in classic hierarchical organisations). However, the need for order and precision, to be in control, micromanagement, and the associated pedantic attitude and risk of excessive sadistic components foster irrational fear and destroy active participation and feedback from others. It can also reinforce bureaucratic structures, which inhibit creativity and autonomy.

The **hysterical type** can appear slightly naïve, excited and energised by new ideas, actively making risky decisions, experiential, not planning ahead, and appearing thus uncommitted, superficial and without depth. The need for freedom *of* something instead of the freedom *for* something (e.g. one can be free of constraints or free for commitment) can make these types act in an anarchic way, where rules and regulations are dismissed and ideas quickly stray from a recently chosen path. Furthermore, these types tend to not adapt well to reality, but rather adapt reality to their own perspective and needs.

Another important leadership type, which does not fit into the above four fields due to its complexity, is the **narcissistic personality**. A growing number of leaders are being diagnosed narcissistic – Kets de Vries and Miller (1984) claimed, "if there is one personality constellation to which leaders tend to gravitate, it is the narcissistic one" (p. 5/6). Narcissism seems to be the driving force behind the desire to obtain a leadership position (Kets de Vries & Miller, 1984) and is arguably a prerequisite for anyone who hopes to rise to the top of an organisation (Kets de Vries & Engellau, 2010). The narcissistic type's intense need for power and prestige drives them to take up leadership roles, yet their leadership is driven by an egotistical desire for power and admiration (Kets de Vries & Miller, 1997) that does not take into account the needs of the organisation or other individuals.

A trait associated with narcissism is the ability to employ charm and create a good impression, hence, narcissists are very good at attaining leadership roles, but they do not necessarily perform well once in the position. Narcissists do however have particular strengths; they can be highly visionary and as such inspire a great number of people (Maccoby, 2000). This fosters loyalty and group identity through strong conviction of the righteousness of their cause, that their group, organisation or country has a special mission. After a while others suffer sadly easily an overdose (Kets de Vries & Engellau, 2010). Narcissists have a large number of weaknesses; they are hypersensitive to criticism due to their (well-hidden) feelings of inferiority, which also leads to an insatiable need for recognition and superiority; they are poor listeners; they lack empathy, can thus be exploitative and depreciatory; they can be highly irrational, angry and inflexible; they are unwilling or unable to mentor or be mentored; and they are intensely competitive (Kernberg, 1984; Maccoby, 2000; Rosenthal, 2006, p. 44). Excessive self-reference and self-centredness, grandiosity and over-evaluation hide the fact that narcissists are overly dependent on external admiration and desire to be loved by their followers. Under severe frustration or without the external admiration they crave, they may develop paranoid trends; they can then become suspicious, sadistically controlling or enraged when interpreting minor opposition as a dangerous rebellion or hidden attack (Kernberg, 1984). Dealing so poorly with criticism, narcissists rarely consult with colleagues, preferring to make decisions on their own. Other risks of derailment are isolation from reality, conflict avoidance, abrasive behaviour, micromanagement, feeling like an impostor and hypomanic behaviour (Kets de Vries & Engellau, 2010). Narcissistic types tend to surround themselves with "yes-men" and are shrewd manipulators (Kets de Vries, 2004), and thus bound to leave damaged systems and relationships in their wake (Rosenthal, 2006). Furthermore, followers might collude unconsciously with their grandiosity, either through the mechanism of identifying with the aggressor or by creating a *folie à deux*, a system of shared madness and delusion (Kets de Vries, 2004). Narcissistic types are "of high intelligence, hardworking, eminently talented or capable, but their narcissistic needs dramatically neutralise or destroy their creative potential for organisations" (Kernberg, 1984, p. 56).

It is extremely helpful for a coach to understand where narcissism stems from in order to gain insight into the concealed suffering of the client. This personality structure can develop from infancy to adulthood when one is unable to integrate the idealised beliefs one has of oneself with the realities of one's inadequacies (Rosenthal, 2006). The gratification needs of healthy narcissism follow those of the normal individual. Normal self-love is mature, enlightened and deep; there is commitment to ideals and values, capacity for love and investment in others without childlike and shallow self-aggrandisement. It incorporates idealism and altruism, shows a tolerance for normal and unavoidable frustrations, and pleasure is gained from helping and seeing the successes of others (Kernberg, 1984). Sadly, pathological narcissists spend their lives seeking recognition from idealised parental substitutes as an emotional salve for their shortcomings (Rosenthal, 2006). However, the pain behind the narcissistic structure is missing here. A deeper understanding may be obtained by looking at Ovid's story of Narcissus. He, a beautiful young man, was adored and loved by many women, but could never himself fall in love. The little nymph Echo had also fallen in love with Narcissus, but just as was the case with the others, he could not develop any feelings for her. In her sorrow, the nymph disappeared, becoming what we know today as the echo. The gods became angry at this and pronounced that Narcissus would fall in love with the next being he saw – alas, he fell in love with his own reflection in a pond from which he intended to drink. Yet whenever he touched his mirror image it disintegrated. This caused Narcissus to himself die of sorrow and be reborn as the narcissus flower.

This means, that the deep need for a mirror and mirroring (because s/he was not sufficiently mirrored and seen by parental figures) and the reaching out for love destroys the capacity of the other to love him or her. Thus, the pain, the desire and the need for love is never satisfied, the fear of not existing unless reflected is continuous. This is a painful situation, treatment is very difficult since the creation of genuine self-esteem and the capacity to love oneself is based on having been mirrored long enough for trust to develop and emotional needs to be met.

In ordinary praxis, coaches should and will not meet mentally ill leaders, yet most of us have unresolved neurotic tendencies. It is therefore helpful to remember the anxieties and goals behind these structures to help clients find their way through their own "behavioural and emotional jungle".

13

Facing challenges such as resistance and defences

In coaching (as well as therapy), clients do not always agree with what the coach proposes or develops as hypothesis. Resistance can be expressed, and often defensive mechanisms can obstruct understanding what exactly it is that is experienced as threatening or destabilising the balance of the psychic system. Resistance and defences can be understood as the person's psychological immune system: they prevent the person from feeling the pain of a threat or from developing unpleasant insight, and at the same time provide clues to the origins of their questions and problems (Messer, 2002).

Resistance, as a very basic phenomenon, can present itself in several forms and for different purposes:

- Resistance to the coaching in general: some clients are sent by their company and do not want to engage with the coaching relationship – from a psychodynamic perspective this can also be explored and discussed in the sessions in an empathic way. One could also clarify what coaching is about and what it offers.
- Resistance to the recognition of impulses, feelings, fantasies and motifs (Messer, 2002) – in coaching we often encounter a resistance to acknowledge negative feelings such as anxiety. Empathising is a useful approach to dealing with this issue, as over the course of time doing so can help the client feel they are understood and make them more willing to open up.
- Resistance in the form of not changing the behaviour outside the room (Messer, 2002) – sometimes behavioural changes require more time and a slow integration process before new insights can be applied in reality.

- Resistance as a function of failure to empathise on the part of the coach – this can result from a lack of attunement to the client that leads to the client feeling misunderstood.

(Messer, 2002)

Resistance can be shown and demonstrated actively or manifest via a defence mechanism kicking in. Freud coined the term "defences" (see Chapter 8) because he was fond of military metaphors and used them in a pedagogical way, and secondly because what he observed as "first-line defences", such as repression and conversion, he understood as processes operating in their defensive function, protecting clients from overwhelming and unpleasant feelings – at the cost of them not living a full life.

Defences develop as healthy and creative adaptations that serve the purpose of protecting the self against powerful negative feelings such as anxiety, grief and other disorganising emotions, or maintaining self-esteem.

When dealing with the boundary of the self and the outer-world, defences are referred to as **primitive or immature (psychotic splitting)**, whereas the higher order defences deal with internal boundaries between the various intrapsychic instances such as Ego, Id and Superego. The level of maturity depends on the psychic cost and unconscious disadvantages of the defence.

At the **higher order level of defences** we find the following mechanisms:

The first involves **non-psychotic splitting**, where the world is split into "good and bad" and "us and them" (e.g. the competitor is seen as "the enemy"), and **projections**, where unwanted or repressed shadow aspects are projected on to another individual. **Projective identification** can occur in a management context and pose a problem, when out of fear and anxiety a personal need for grandiosity is so strongly projected onto, for example the CEO, that s/he begins to identify with the projection and picture themselves as, e.g. a corporate hero or grandiose rescuer (see Chapter 8).

More mature mechanisms are **intellectualising, rationalising and affect isolation**, which suppress emotional aspects (intellectualising), invent rational arguments (rationalising), and cause feelings to become unconscious (affect isolation) and give way to cognitive and rational aspects.

Repression is the first defence Freud encountered, and is one of the most basic, where psychic content (names, places, situations) are (actively) forgotten or ignored to prevent disturbing or painful thoughts becoming conscious.

Displacement means redirecting an impulse (mostly aggressive) to a target it was not initially influenced by (i.e. telling off a partner instead of the boss).

Reaction formation is linked to the human capacity to turn something into its opposite; converting a negative affect into a positive one, and vice versa. For example, longing is transformed to contempt, envy to attraction, hatred to love.

Turning against the self involves redirecting aggression towards another person/an external object towards one self, so that one thinks, for example, that an external problem is one's own fault.

Undoing is a process whereby an affect of anger, guilt or shame is unconsciously counterbalanced by an attitude or behaviour that will erase the former (i.e. unconsciously giving a gift to a person with which one has previously experienced an emotionally difficult situation).

Denial is the refusal to accept the reality of an unpleasant experience. Denial can have a practical purpose when a life-threatening event is experienced, as it allows us to continue functioning regardless of the pain caused by the event.

The most active and mature mechanism is **humour**, a recourse in response to difficult emotional situations that arise in interaction with others which is actively used to de-stress and cope with outer- and inner-conflicts.

Sublimation refers to transforming internal conflicts into creative and socially acceptable solutions; it has entered daily language in reference to the work of artists or other creative people.

All these defences can take on different shades and variations; they play a part in a healthy reaction or solidify it to a personality trait or disorder – as always, it is a matter of degree (see Mentzos, 2009).

The objective of **dealing with a client's defences** is to unblock the person from an unhelpful or even destructive reaction pattern and allow them the freedom to choose a suitable response instead of falling into an automated reaction-trap. Working with (the more mature) defences and complexes can be rewarding for the client in the sense that it enriches the behavioural repertoire by facilitating the development of new attitudes and reactions towards psychic threats. Kets de Vries describes this as the **"restructuring of the inner theatre"** consisting of defences, emotions and self-perception. **Defences** are restructured by recognising them, understanding them, giving up excessive defensive patterns and developing new coping mechanisms. **Affective** restructuring takes place on the level of emotional patterns – how people feel emotions and express them – by developing reaction alternatives, which imply a change in emotion. On the level of **self-perception**, the way people perceive themselves in relation to others can be changed, especially when dysfunctional patterns create negative self-perceptions and thus hinder interpersonal exchange, by supporting self-esteem and a positive and realistic self-perception (Kets de Vries, 2006).

The Jungian perspective on psychic threats is built around the notion of **complexes** and archetypes. Defences are understood as the expression of the self-regulatory functioning of the psyche finding a constructive means of managing difficult situations. Analytical psychology assumes that the psyche has a built-in compensatory function, where too little in one area produces too much in another. Since conscious and unconscious are also understood as compensatory, a psychological crisis is healed by uniting and integrating opposites, such as good and bad or light and shadow, in the totality of the Self. In the **individuation process**, psychic energy is directed towards the achievement of wholeness and is controlled and driven by the Self.

Complexes consist of conflicting or opposing poles of one psychic aspect. For example the inferiority complex – with its opposing poles of nothingness and omnipotence – has entered into every-day language. Jung understood complexes as unconscious psychic contents held together by one emotion and a common core of meaning, relating to an archetype, that can be charged with a high degree of positive or negative emotional energy. A negative complex may be the product of a deeply felt negative emotional event, psychological trauma or negative childhood experiences. As "split off components of the psyche" (Jung, 1934), complexes may cause psychic disturbances in the unconscious and block psychic energy via "ward-off" processes. Through its archetypal core, the symptoms of a complex can be understood and interpreted symbolically. In a coaching situation, seeking the symbolic meaning provides a playful and non-threatening approach to developing an understanding, since it does not focus on pathologies; the focus lies not with eliminating the possibly neurotic conflict, but on learning to bear and live with it. This enables the release of the psychic energy bound in the defence – psychic equilibrium and inner-balance can be re-established, and an instant of personality integration occurs.

14

Working with defences on the group and organisational level

Coaching always takes place in a systemic context where individuals work together to achieve the overall organisational purpose and goal – independent of whether the coach works with the individual or the team (see Chapter 9). Understanding defences at a group level is thus also a necessary competency for the psychodynamic coach. They defend the group-as-a-whole against unpleasant emotions resulting from threats such as growing uncertainty.

One way of looking at **defences at the group level** is through **the lens of ego-defences**. Based on the idea that a group must maintain and enhance a shared self-esteem and conserve and protect organisational or group identity, Brown and Starkey (2000) refer to social defences such as denial, rationalisation, idealisation, phantasy[1] and symbolisation. These are understood to hinder organisational and group learning and are thus counterproductive to the necessary development and decision-making processes – as they are always based on processing and applying new information in the present context. Although for systematic reasons these defences are discussed separately in the literature, they tend to appear together and reinforce each other.

Organisational symbols can distort or conceal reality and restrict the capacity to perceive and process information. As symbols in this defensive sense, myths, uniforms, titles and hierarchies may be recognised for their soothing and reassuring capacity (Brown & Starkey, 2000).

Cultural (and organisational) complexes (Kimbles & Singer, 2004) can also be understood as a defence against the repetition of a former trauma or discrimination which has been anchored in the collective unconscious of a group. If stirred up, these past experiences can engross the (group's) collective psyche, whereby the cultural unconscious captures perceptions, behavioural patterns and feelings that follow their own logic.

Upholding existing belief structures and collectively **denying that a problem** exists is a common defence, so too is **rationalisation**. The latter is the most important ingredient of **groupthink**, whereas **phantasy** and **idealisation** are the common ground for Bion's basic assumptions.

Janis (1972) introduced the term **"groupthink"**, by which he depicts a "premature concurrence seeking behaviour" that results in defective information search and evaluation processes and is borne of stress and anxiety (Chapman, 2006). With "groupthink", Janis describes the concept of the *decision trap*, which he observed having taken place in specific political events. He found that in the decision-making situations leading to the invasion of Pearl Harbor, the Watergate affair, the Vietnam war and the North Korean war, the decision-making group made bad or at least unrealistic decisions. This outcome was perceived to be due to the fact that every member of the decision committee was subject to a supposed group opinion and hence held back their own viewpoint so as not to upset the ostensible harmony. Janis claims that in specific situations characterised by cohesion, isolation, high stress levels and strong leadership, behavioural factors such as self-censorship, peer pressure, the illusion of invulnerability and simplified reductions of reality result in possible alternatives being overlooked, and as a consequence, the decisions made are far removed from reality. Groupthink has become a widely, unfortunately often imprecisely, used term for negative group dynamics in decision situations involving managers and politicians; however, more recent research questions the details of this theory and the test results (for summaries see, e.g. Chapman, 2006; Rose, 2011).

Less well known in the wider public sphere, but interesting from a psychodynamic perspective is Bion's discovery of the **basic assumption mode**. Taken from a naïve psychological perspective, when in this mode, group members will assume both what they should do and what they are implicitly expected to do (Ettin et al., 1997, p. 332). Bion designated these observed collective patterns "cultures" or "mentalities" (French & Simposn, 2010). The group functions as a work group on a conscious and more rational plane, whereas on a less conscious and less rational plane, the members experience and enact the elements of the basic assumption culture or mentality.

The **work group mentality** is concerned with completing the primary task, while at the same time consciously and effectively dealing with the emotions that arise within and from this process. Confronting factual and emotional reality is part of dealing with the primary task and is an important aspect of leadership. When the leader and/or the structures, rules and regulations do an inadequate job of containing underlying anxieties, when there are no opportunities to discuss and work through worries and trepidations, group level social defences can set in to transform and neutralise strong tensions and affects, thereby dealing with negative emotions and allowing the group to remain unthreatened.

The terms **"basic assumption group"** and "work group" do not signify people but "facets of mental activity in a group . . . only mental activity of a particular kind, not people who indulge in it" (Bion, 1961, pp. 143–144). To make this distinction more explicit, French and Simpson (2010) propose the terms "basic assumption mentality" and "work group mentality". Both mentalities co-exist; however, one will prevail over the other. When a group shifts away from the primary task and the work group mentality to a basic assumption mentality, group members may not realise this shift and even think that the work atmosphere has improved. If a group member detects a pattern and shares this insight with other group members, they will most likely be ignored or attacked, hence the basic assumption mentality will prevail (French & Simpson, 2010). Table 14.1 provides an overview of known basic assumption mentalities.

To explain the table: through regression to collective unconscious fantasies (first column), members create a "new" (unconscious) group identity and mentality (second column) from a combination of defence mechanisms (third column) to deal with a specific set of emotions (fourth column) which can support or hinder achievement

Table 14.1 An overview of basic assumption mentalities

Collective phantasy	Basic assumption mentality	Dominant defence mechanism	Dominant affect
Dependency	The leader should feed and protect	Idealisation of the leader or his "word"	Depression, jealousy, guilt, worship
Pairing	Resulting from the pairing of two group members, something new, a new idea/person will rid the group of destruction, hate and hopelessness	Phantasies via a utopian ideal	Hope, trust, enthusiasm, despair, disillusion
Fight-Flight	The existence of an external enemy, who necessitates fight, defence or flight	Projection and splitting	Anger, hate, fear, moments of suspicion
One-ness	Powerful connection with an almighty power, an oceanic feeling of unity	Denial of individual differences	Identity fears and conflicts, fragmentation, animosity
Me-ness	The individual's inner-world becomes a place of comfort. The group does not exist	Splitting and projection in society	Fear of destruction and loss of self, sadism, passive aggression
Group-formation	The group oscillates between one-ness and me-ness	Attacks on alliances and integrative attempts	Threat to the group identity and individual identity

Source: Nagel (2014, p. 108, adapted from Kinzel, 2002)

of the primary goal. This arising basic assumption mentality may be either short lived or persist as the dominant mode (Bion, 1961). Although originally intended to mitigate emotional threats, basic assumptions can over time become dysfunctional and bureaucratic, since they not only reduce anxiety, but also replace compassion, empathy, awareness and meaning with control and impersonality (Kets de Vries, 2004). As a consequence, the perception of reality becomes distorted and decision-making is impaired.

Understanding the social defences the client uses in their organisation is important for two reasons. First, the client might be the leader of a group or organisation, and as such their role will demand the ability to detect the mentalities operating in the work context so as to better understand which emotional needs of the group are not being met (e.g. a need to be inspired, protected, nurtured, developed, etc.). Here it is also necessary for the leader to be aware of their own contribution to the dominant basic assumption mentality. As Ettin et al. (1997) describe, groups have "an uncanny knack for finding leaders who manifest latent group dynamics and thereby find their niche and sources of power". Ultimately, it is the leader who is responsible for accomplishing the primary task. Second, when coaching a member of a group, it can be helpful to understand the destructive forces acting on the individual which are exercised by the basic assumption mentality, the individual's contribution to the basic assumption mode and the personal inner-hook connected to this.

In attempting to detect these unconscious group patterns, it can be constructive to analyse the **parallel process between the client and the coach**. This concept stems from the use of supervision in psychotherapy (see Searles, 1955). Searles found, that the process of reflection between patient and therapist is mirrored in the relationship between therapist and supervisor. Through this re-enactment, the supervisor can develop an understanding of and an insight into the psychological process of the patient. The parallel process is based on transference and countertransference as well as projective identification. Applying this concept to the coaching relationship with the client, a parallel process in the relationship between the client and the coach can mirror the defences enacted in the respective work group or organisation. This requires the coach to be capable of dual-listening and entails the dilemma of whom does the coach work for: the organisation, or the client?

Note

1 Phantasy is a technical term than the commonly used word "fantasy" which tends to denote notions of whimsy or eccentricity. In psycho-analytic thinking unconscious phantasies are the driving force of all significant human subjective experience (Laplanche & Pontalis, 1972).

15

Being aware of risks and limitations

The risks inherent in working within a relationship and with the emotions of the client are manifold and must be kept in mind by the coach. The work entails the creation of a secure base (Bowlby, 1988), a holding environment from which the client can open up freely, share and explore anxieties and worries, and develop new insights and creative solutions without clinging to defences. This requires clear time boundaries and a suitable physical space. Difficult emotions and situations also call for a non-judgemental attitude, reliability, genuine interest in the client and a set of professional skills based on thorough training.

Psychic risks for the client

Emotional dependency can develop from a client's situation characterised by a lack of secure attachment, be it biographical or in the context of the organisational setup. The latter might occur more often in modern organisations where either hierarchies are too dissolved or leaders are not capable of or willing to create a secure environment. In this instance, the client could then assign the coach as an attachment figure. Of course, in a positive client-coach relationship, positive transference supports the developmental process for the client and is a necessary ingredient – yet an inappropriate dependency will torpedo the developmental process, holding the client in a regressive and immature state.

Unconscious collusions between the coach and the client are part of the mutual learning process, and their appearance – when detected by the coach – provides an insight into the defences and emotional reactions of the client. Supervision is therefore a helpful tool that the coach can use to reflect on transference, countertransference and the relationship with the client. However, when these collusions go undetected, either because the coach is not under supervision or is not willing to reflect on their own psychic system, they can reinforce the existing patterns of the client and disguise the underlying psychological dynamics. In such a situation, the coaching process would not contribute to positive psychic development.

Clients may have experienced traumatising events involving emotionally significant individuals. A traumatising event can be completely encapsulated in the psychic system and repressed by a system of defences. When the coach is not sufficiently trained, does not show due care, or misreads psychic signals, **re-traumatisation** may occur due to an insistence on "pulling down" the defences, even though they serve to protect the client and allow them to live a normal life. Opening this psychic wound will not only hurt the client, it may render them incapable of functioning in their work role. If the coach does not have a strong enough psychological background or sufficient training to hold the client, it is recommended that the client be referred to a psychotherapist.

Since the title is not protected, anyone with or without proper training can call themselves a (psychodynamic) coach. An open market such as this attracts charlatans and those working for their own benefit and agenda. In such cases, the client's developmental process can be endangered by **emotional abuse and manipulative behaviour** from the side of the coach. For the sake of their own psyche, the client should ask the coach to provide training certificates to verify that they possess the basic level of competence necessary to work with this relationship-based approach.

Psychic risks for the coach

In transference, projective identification poses a problem; the client may project their need for grandiosity or devaluation on to the coach, who may then unconsciously identify with these projections. Undifferentiated and unrecognised narcissistic or masochistic needs of the coach might make this identification possible and may harm their psychological health. This demonstrates well how important it is for the coach to recognise their own psychic tendencies and patterns so that they can differentiate between their own psychic system and that of the client.

Temptations can arise from social defences at the work group or organisational level. The basic assumption mentality pairing might seduce the coach and the client into this mode. Not only might it feed into the pride and narcissistic needs of the coach, it may also jeopardise the effectiveness of the group's work. This unconscious need for pairing may not only be expressed on the work level, it may also manifest through a friendship or sexual relationship. These unconscious forces can be very seductive, yet adherence to work ethics on the part of the coach should prevent them from prevailing. Besides the challenges presented by this pairing, a coach might also feel inclined to become part of the organisation, especially when there is a leadership vacuum which addresses the coach's unconscious or conscious need to be a leader.

Further risks are highlighted by the question, who **sponsors the client relationship**, is it the organisation, or is it the client? This presents a dilemma for the coach concerning whom to address should a psychopathological aspect reveal itself, or in case the client wants to leave the organisation during or after the coaching. Is it for instance necessary to reveal the pathological aspect or the intention to quit to the organisation? What kind of confidentiality agreement was reached and up to which degree of pathology must it be adhered to? To whom does the coach owe which obligations? These are very important questions from the practical perspective and will be further discussed in the next section.

The fact that psychodynamic coaching has evolved from psychoanalysis and psychotherapy contributes to the **limitations** of this approach. It entails the risk that the coach places too much emphasis on the problem and not enough on the strengths and creative competencies of the client. The coach therefore must support and commemorate achievements as well as value and build on the client's strengths and existing capabilities.

The depth of this coaching approach is not always wanted or needed by the client, however. Often, clients are seeking short-term, pragmatic interventions that do not question underlying patterns and structures. For the more explorative and developmentally oriented client, psychodynamic coaching has proven to be very effective. For quick and short engagements it is certainly not a useful framework (Lee, 2014).

Practice Part I

PREPARING FOR THE CLIENT

In this section we will introduce practical aspects of the coaching work along the developmental timeline of a coaching relationship. Before we dive into general questions such as how to run a coaching session, we will first focus our attention on the practical foundations of psychodynamic coaching and how to prepare for the client by exploring the setting and the implicit and explicit attitudes and assumptions of the client and coach. Another aspect of preparation for the coaching relationship that will be covered here is contracting. As the contract can be made with an organisation or an individual, it can be understood as a first intervention and diagnostic phase.

16

Assumptions for the coach regarding the client

Coaching based on psychodynamics implies a number of non-trivial assumptions regarding the client and the understanding of the client's mind, as well as the practical characteristics of the coach's task (see also Sandler, 2011).

The unconscious exists

Psychodynamic coaching distinguishes itself from other coaching approaches through the assumption that **the unconscious exists** and is represented in unconscious thoughts and feelings, and that emotional experiences, conscious as well as unconscious, are significant in that they influence our thoughts and actions.

Making the unconscious conscious

The central objective of psychodynamic coaching is to make the unconscious conscious – it aspires to support the client in becoming aware of how limiting and dysfunctional unconscious thought patterns can be and how this self-awareness can foster freedom and a broader bandwidth of behavioural and emotional reactions.

Fear and other emotions

Crucial to this work is the understanding of emotions, particularly anxiety – one of the most unwanted, unpleasant and tabooed emotions despite its necessary signalling function. This implies that

working with mostly unpleasant emotions such as anger, anxiety, guilt, fear and shame can be psychologically painful for the client – this is a far from simple process. The unearthing of unconscious material which is emotionally laden and has been hidden for good reason behoves the guidance of specifically trained coaches who have a sensitivity to hidden psychic risks and "shallow waters" and are capable of creating a psychological and physical holding environment. Notwithstanding, it is crucial to allow the re-activation of inner-resources, to celebrate achievements and also use humour to ease the acceptance of challenging insights and to avoid being preoccupied by problems only.

Unsolved internal and external conflicts

Whether conscious or unconscious, unresolved internal and external conflicts hinder psychic and therefore personal and professional development. They shall be detected, worked with and, ideally, solved. Very often these conflicts are concealed by individual and social defence mechanisms – and if solidified may bring about dysfunctional emotional and behavioural patterns. These patterns represent how we regulate emotions and are based on early relationships with attachment figures; they contribute to the brain routines that understand and manage relationships.

Relationships

Relationships are key: they form the world we live in, they are our foundation for everything we do, think and feel – be it past relationships with caregivers or any other important relationships in the past or present. Understanding the client's typical relationship patterns is a crucial coaching endeavour. The coach may use transference and countertransference phenomena to decipher these patterns and to support the client in developing greater self-awareness and lessening dysfunctional reactions. While some psychodynamic coaches dive into past relationships as part of their working method, others only deal with the here and now of the client's life. In either case, working with relationships is an essential ingredient of psychodynamic coaching, where the emphasis is on the development of personal and human capabilities rather than technical skills.

On the client side, the requisite mentalising capacity may be limited in instances where the client feels emotionally excited or threatened or due to the impact of mental disorders such as depression or substance abuse. Attending to a client in such a condition demands a balancing act on the part of the coach, whereby s/he must keep one foot in the client's emotional system and the other outside it in order to observe and contemplate the actual situation. One of the "leitmotifs" of coaching is the client developing an empathic relationship with themselves (Lawrence, 2006); clients must learn to live with their personal weaknesses and to be kind to themselves.

When the client enters into a coaching agreement, as part of the contracting phase, clarification on these assumptions and working concepts is essential.

17

Assumptions for the coach regarding themselves – attitude, perspective and training

Assumptions regarding the functioning of the mind call for a specific attitude and duty of care on the part of the coach. When dealing with the vulnerabilities of the client and the psychological risks of derailment, it is extremely important for coaches to understand what they should bring to the table and what problems they may encounter.

Interest in human beings and their truth together with a not-knowing attitude

A genuine **interest in human beings and their individual truth** brings about an attitude of veracity for the wellbeing of the client, whereby the coach clarifies any subjectivity and questions assumptions, whether they be individual, organisational or cultural. This genuine interest also implies that the coach shall be a good, attentive, curious, non-critical and non-judgemental listener. A mindset that is open to exploration is crucial to conveying the essential **attitude of not-knowing**. Only when the coach's not-knowing disposition is authentic and experienced as such can creative or even painful insights be experimented with, reflected upon and tested to find the client's individual truth. It is important to refrain from being too hasty and jumping on seemingly obvious explications prematurely. For coaches who are very solution or advice oriented, this might seem counterintuitive and not in keeping with their personal style – these coaches should reconsider whether psychodynamic coaching will fit into their repertoire. The attitude of not-knowing relates also to the question of whether the coach shall share personal stories and experiences. From a psychodynamic perspective this is not advisable; however, clients do sometimes respond well to personal "war-stories" as their sharing helps them feel "equal" to the coach. The risk here is that the client may feel misunderstood or misinterpreted; reacting badly to an important detail being mistaken or taking the story too personally without any further exploration. As always, the task of the coach is finding the right balance.

Own vulnerabilities

When working with clients it is crucial for the coach to recognise their **own vulnerabilities**, basic emotional and behavioural patterns and major defensive tendencies – this presents an important stage of the psychodynamic training process. The purpose of this is not only to develop empathy with the other and oneself, but also to understand one's own vulnerabilities and not confuse one's own feelings and difficulties with those of the client. Only once this has been established can countertransference be successfully integrated in the work (see Chapter 8).

Empathy

Only those who perceive and understand their own feelings can **empathise** with others. Kohut (1966) describes empathy as "a single act to capture secure knowledge of complex psychic configurations (in another person)". It is a means of immersing oneself in the world of the other, stepping into their shoes without totally abandoning one's own point of view. Neuroscience has shown that when sharing other people's emotions, the same neuronal structures are addressed as if you were experiencing them yourself. Parts of this process are "automatic", so to speak, but attention, context, conscious change of perspective and the quality of the relationship with the other influence empathy (Singer & Lamm,

2009). Compassion or sympathy, which differ from empathy in the sense that they refer to an awareness of the other's suffering but not suffering directly as if one were the other, are also necessary, as is mentalising, which is the attentive observation and reflection of one's own behaviour and that of others through the attribution of mental states (see Chapter 11).

A holding and containing environment

When clients share their feelings, especially their anxieties and their failures, they must do so within a **secure environment**. Feelings of safety and security are derived from a safe physical space and a non-judgemental, non-critical, open-minded attitude on the part of the coach. The concept of the holding environment is based on Winnicott's idea of the *holding mother* (1965), which in the coaching context translates into offering a responsive, attuned and flexible tuning in to the client's emotional needs. Containment can go one step further – hereby the coach can help the client to digest painful insights by pre-conceptualising and reframing them so that they can more easily be taken in by the client. Meaning can emerge through a process of co-creation, but clients may not have the capacity to own their feelings and emotions. Hence, the task for the coach is to hold these feelings and emotions, reflect on them and hand them back to the client when appropriate (Pooley, 2006).

Transference and countertransference

The coach can either function as a projective surface onto which the client **transfers** feelings that stem from a re-enactment of another relationship, most often relationships with parental figures and caregivers, or observe transference within the client's description of their own behaviour towards others in the work context. Training and supervision focussing on self-awareness and self-reflection is necessary to properly recognise this transference.

Countertransference, in contrast, can only be experienced by the coach – this task of feeling the client's unfelt feelings without confusing them with personal emotional states is one of the most difficult a coach will face. This very specific function requires time to develop and will do so from reflection on real-life coaching cases under supervision. An understanding solely acquired through textbooks or presentations will not be sufficient.

Transitional thinking

The coaching relationship must provide a safe space in which the client can reflect on and change their behaviour, thinking and feeling. **Transitional thinking** (Spero, 2006) asserts that coaching provides a transitional space for the client within which they can experiment with themselves; a space not only of safety, but also a creative space that can incorporate both reality and non-reality. This space is characterised by feelings of attachment and separation, as well as dependency and independency, and is conducive to play, imagination and invention. Through a "creative metaphoric approach" (Lawrence, 2006), unconscious thoughts can emerge in the transitional space and develop into a new perspective on life and oneself, as a human being per se and within the organisational setting.

Respect defences

When working with unconscious material it is essential throughout all phases of the coaching process to have **respect for the unconscious** and its effects. Psychic defence systems have a reason to be, and the goal should not be to disable them, per se, as they serve the purpose of protecting the person from feeling emotional pain. Pain is not only unpleasant and uncomfortable, it can also be unbearable. Destroying these boundaries and hence creating a vulnerability to re-traumatisation must be strictly avoided in a coaching situation. The unconscious – metaphorically speaking – can be very constructive in finding ways of looking at life and its experiences, but it can also be very destructive, as nightmares, psychotic reactions and anxiety disorders demonstrate. Respect for the unconscious comprises respect for the human being, its joys, its sufferings and its limitations.

Training and perfection

It is essential for a psychodynamic coach to undergo proper practical and theoretical psychodynamic training. Theory can certainly be learnt through textbooks, but working in praxis with the psychodynamic approach requires prior training with clients under supervision as well as self-experience within a coaching or therapy setting. The basic capacities discussed in this chapter shall be explored and improved.

One final remark regarding the coach and their work concerns the search for perfection, which seems to pervade contemporary society. In working with clients this can be rather detrimental, as it counteracts an ambience of engaging, playful and experimental learning and development. Winnicott (1965) coined the term **"good enough"** to express that a parental figure being good enough and not perfect *is* more than good enough (Pooley, 2006). Making and accepting mistakes, not-(yet)knowing, and even premature comments are not only permitted, but required for the coach to become part of the transitional space.

18

The general setting

Place

An ideal setting for this work would be a designated coaching room that is private, quiet and free of disturbance – a contrast from the client's daily setting, it should be well-furnished and provide a comfortable ambiance. It is helpful to have a flipchart and refreshments available. No phones will ring – we should be secluded from any intrusion or disturbance. The position of the seating also plays a role. Client and coach should be able to see each other without being forced to sit face-to-face. A good solution is to position two turnable chairs at a slight angle with a small table in between; this arrangement offers the coach the ability to observe the client without creating discomfort (Beck, 2012). Allowing the client the choice of where to sit and change positions if they so desire is important as, beyond helping the client feel at ease, it may also offer hints as to what is going on within the client's psyche. I have also conducted coaching sessions whilst walking with the client. Walking is conducive to a free flow of ideas and can be very helpful to the coaching. Other coaches meet in the office or meeting room of the client, or more public spaces such as cafés, restaurants and hotel lobbies, some even exercise together with the client (e.g. jogging or cycling). I personally find these public settings problematic due to the possibility of compromising confidentiality and privacy, and if possible I prefer to work from my own coaching room, where everything is set up in a way that helps the client feel at ease.

When the client is not physically present, one may also use the phone, Skype or Zoom to conduct the coaching sessions – yet it is recommended to meet the client for the first time and every now and then in person. Transference and countertransference are easier to experience face to face.

Duration and interval

There are no rules set in stone but, for the client, coming together for one hour after arriving from a very different setting during the day is difficult. In most cases, it takes executives a degree of time to put their professional duties and restraints behind them and open up and dive into their inner-world. A minimum of two, and up to three or four hours, are possible durations for coaching sessions. Some coaches even devote an entire day to working with a client. The interval also depends on the client's needs and abilities. If the time interval grows too long, for example several months, the coach will have difficulty tuning in with the client and recalling the previous sessions, yet if it is too short, the client may encounter problems in freeing-up sufficient time. Based on my experience, an interval of between three to six weeks works best.

19

Contracting – the very first meeting

First contact and diagnostics

The first contact can take place between the potential client and the coach, or both parties together with a representative of the organisation. Sometimes contact with the sponsoring organisation precedes the first meeting with the client. In any case, these first meetings serve the purpose of establishing whether the people in the room could see themselves working together on the coaching task. Chemistry, intuitive reactions towards each other, first impressions, aspects of trust, ways of talking, speaking the same language, behaviour – in both directions, these factors will determine whether or not a coaching contract will be signed. At the same time, this initial encounter is the first diagnostic stage whereby the coach must carefully observe the situation, the people involved and, most importantly, personal feelings and countertransference (best practice is to take notes during or immediately after the meeting). Similar to the concept of the "now moment" (Stern) or the "initial dream" (Jung), the first meeting can contain in a nutshell the whole story of the client, and the major issues. Its unfolding will take place over the course of the work and only at the end will one be able to fully realise what was inherent from the very beginning.

Setting the scene

While the coach must remain highly alert, sensitive to every little detail, accessible and non-judgemental, at the same time s/he has to be setting boundaries, preparing and creating the implicit and explicit work contract out of a position of natural authority, equality and respect. The latter leads on to the process of setting the scene for the coaching.

When working with an individual, some coaches will establish a contract based on an hourly fee structure, similar to how clients attending private therapy are charged. Of course, other payment structures such as coaching packages can be applied, which may entail working together face to face for a pre-determined length of time, with additional support being provided through other means such as phone or Skype, etc. For organisational clients, some coaches combine different coaching and communication tools and create a bundle price, e.g. six months coaching including the diagnostic interview, twenty hours face-to-face coaching, email coaching and urgent phone calls limited to twenty minutes each time for a price of x euros. There are no limitations to how these payment terms can be structured. Packages simplify liquidity planning for the coach and organisational clients are accustomed to them – ultimately it is a question of personal preference.

Rules

When an organisation "sends" an individual for coaching, it is necessary to clearly establish roles and responsibilities before the process commences. For example, will there be conversations between the organisation's representative and the coach? If, so, under what terms? Will these conversations be prepared in the coaching session? Or will conversation only be permitted when all three parties are sat at the table? Clarity on **confidentiality** is critical, and in a triangular relationship the risk of splitting and divergence is immanently present (Huffington, p. 99). Another necessity is establishing how the coaching relationship will be **evaluated**. As professionalisation grows, client expectations become more demanding, and requests for proof of evidence, efficiency and respective training certificates so that methods and ways of working become more transparent are common.

In preparation of the final contract, financial details as well as contract rules and regulations are recorded. However, the client's concerns and goals should not be included in the contract, too high is the risk for abuse within the organisational system. Yet, defining the goal and how achievement will be measured shall be part of the contracting phase and should be noted by both the coach and the client.

RUNNING THE COACHING SESSIONS

Working from a psychodynamic perspective does not demand strict adherence to one technique or intervention approach. The array of instruments, techniques, means of working, ways of opening and closing sessions, and ways of beginning and ending the relationship are as broad as the described theoretical background. Here I will depict different approaches to "the coaching" as well as share my personal experiences – the point is that there is no right or wrong approach, as long as one works within the assumptions mentioned in Chapters 3, 16 and 17.

20

Beginning the relationship – ways of opening

Although it is rarely the case that the coaching and working relationship starts with the first session, for the sake of descriptive practicality we will assume here that an initial "chemistry" meeting has already taken place.

Goals for the first hours

The first goal is creating a **working alliance** between the coach and client, based on a relationship between two people who have mutually agreed to a basic notion of trust and sympathy. From this hopefully positive starting point the relationship shall develop into an area where the client dares to open up and share their inner- and outer-world, and where the coach feels authorised to support the client in their developmental process. Developing empathy, offering affirmation and understanding, and creating a holding environment are all ways in which the coach can create an atmosphere that is conducive to a first step in this direction.

From a content perspective, the opening hour(s) of the coaching relationship facilitate the development of a **first impression** of the client's major concerns and issues. Discerning invisible obstacles is part of this first step – whether the coach will go ahead or wait to share their insights depends on the client's psychic situation. The opening meetings are important in terms of diagnostics. When the chemistry meeting has been very short or has taken place with a number of people present, the first working meeting is crucial. As already described, this "now moment" (Stern), similar to the "initial dream" (Jung) (see Chapter 19), may unconsciously contain the whole story, the major "symptoms" and the issues behind the "symptom". It might present the basic question or problem in a very condensed way, so that the gestures, behaviours and first sentences paint the essence of the inner-world of the client. The attention to detail in observing the client, countertransference and transference will contribute to a first draft or a first hypothesis of what is really going on in the client's inner-world, and also in the organisation's inner-world. Taking detailed notes either during or shortly after the session will help the coach to revisit these first hours and to further explore the working hypothesis – first as a silent hypothesis, and later together with the client.

Unstructured openings

When practising an **unstructured approach to opening** up the work with a client, no guiding questions are asked, and the client is given no tasks to fulfil. An unstructured and open question such as "Where and how shall we start?" invites the client to express their priorities. It gives the client the freedom to choose where to begin, how to begin, what to talk about, what to share and what not to share. Following an unstructured approach, the coach may not even ask an opening question, and upon greeting and welcoming the client, simply sit and wait for the client to talk. This represents a very orthodox psychoanalytic style and may frighten an unexperienced client, yet this first moment of anxiety can bring the key subject directly to the table. However, opening questions such as "Is there any particular situation/problem/question/insight you would want to start with/ share with me to get started?" allow the client to set the tone and pace of the work. This supports the aspect of equality between the client and the coach, where the coach is less the knowing, consulting expert and more the open, receptive and reflective mirror for the client. Even in cases where the client's organisation has already chosen the basic coaching theme, this open approach hands authority over to the professional and private life back to the individual as client.

Structured openings

Structure can help the client to tune in to a new coaching situation. It reduces complexity, uncertainty and thus anxiety. Which approach is chosen depends not only on the client, but also on the coach's personality and background. A highly structured approach may commence by looking at organisational feedback the client brings to the coaching session (see Chapter 21).

Asking the client to share their **life-story**, be this the tale of their professional life, relationships or a more general overview, gives the client the freedom of choice where to start. I find it useful to develop a basic understanding of where and how the client grew up, the actual emotional quality of their relationships with their parents and siblings as well as how these relationships developed over the years. In sharing these aspects of the life-story, the client not only turns their attention, maybe for the first time, to their feelings regarding important, non-romantic relationships, they also start to open up to their own inner-world. This allows the coach to begin to experience and tune in to some of the client's emotional facets and patterns.

A very different, insightful approach is to let the client express either the problem, the question, the situation in the organisation or the life stage by **painting or drawing** it. This invitation to draw something important can be integrated into the person-in-role or the person-role-system/organisation approach (see Chapter 3). Many years ago I participated in a workshop conducted by Susan Long, who proposed encouraging the client to draw their major roles in life – from early childhood to the present day – without using words. I have been using this approach ever since and find it extremely helpful in connecting the roles with the life-story and developing a first understanding of inherent patterns; linking the different roles, observing and interpreting colours, expressions, reductions, space and later also the omitted, unpainted aspects. The advantage of working with this drawing of roles is that the life-story develops structure and by this containment is created. It also offers the opportunity to revisit the drawing, the different roles and the different interpretations later in the coaching process – it can be a understood as a golden thread for the coaching process.

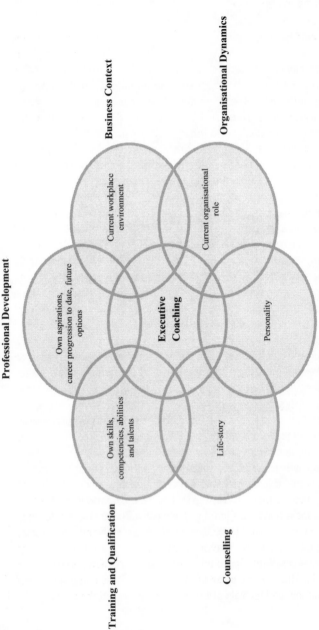

Figure 20.1 The Six-Domain model of executive coaching

Source: Adapted from Brunning (2006, p. 133)

Brunning (2006) proposes a **Six-Domain model**, based on the Person–Role–System model, to work with the client on an emotional contract in specifying which areas to focus on (Figure 20.1).

Brunning denominates these six domains as building blocks for her coaching, since they are simultaneously present during the coaching process. She also suggests that they be viewed as interlinked, for example as cogwheels that have disrupting or harmonising effects on the adjacent wheels. The coach must be reasonably knowledgeable across the board, as it is necessary for them to have the capacity to "become meta to all domains" (p. 135).

Expertise and the relationship

Although the psychodynamic approach is characterised by the specific attitude towards the client, of which not-knowing is an essential part, the degree of orthodoxy will differ depending on the personality of the coach and also the client's situation. In a perfect world, coach and client would be equal, no hierarchy would develop, and both parties would have a commensurate say and contribution. In reality, this ideal is rarely achieved, yet it may not even be necessary to achieve it. Coach and client have different expertise; where the coach has undergone psychodynamic training and has gained psychodynamic knowledge, has experience in coaching and maybe also leadership, the client will always be the expert on their own life and situation, their emotions and their resonance. That being said, mutual respect and recognition of the respective expertise will contribute to mutual trust developing over time.

The understanding of the relationship with the client can change during the coaching session and over the course of the relationship, and vary from a consulting relationship with psychological expertise, a classical working alliance, a shared reflective space, a temporary "shared bath in the unconscious" (see Chapter 11), to a healing situation where painful emotional patterns may be worked through and changed. These different degrees of relationship intensity and personal involvement are all possible. There are no clear rules except that the client is the owner of the situation, and the role of the coach is to support the client.

21

The integration of additional diagnostic tools

Performance measurements

Particularly when dealing with organisations as clients or when the client has been "sent" by the organisation, tools which reflect the performance of the client are used as a point of reference for the coaching goal. These tools can represent a powerful means of engaging with the client's reality and priorities (Kwiatkowski, 2006, p. 154) and can help to adapt, calibrate and attune the coach's behaviour to the personality of the client. This can be advantageous when time is limited yet entails the danger of prematurely framing the means of working with the client. Furthermore, it may induce a false assumption that written (test and report) data are fact, when they could in reality be artefacts that must be examined carefully with that in mind and integrated differently into the coaching process; as artefacts they could be viewed from a symbolic perspective and understood from an organisational culture and defence system point of view.

Annual feedback, evaluation or bonus meetings confront the client with an official external performance appraisal from the organisational world. These assessment tools vary from an informal conversation between the person and their supervisor to an online tool such as a questionnaire which has to be filled out by both parties. Very often this appraisal process is not taken seriously, hence the information acquired is limited. Yet, when supervisor and client collaborate, this can contribute useful new perspectives to the coaching process by identifying areas of high or low performance and thus reveal the client's blind spots or "pain points". It may also help to better understand and appreciate the client's strengths. From a practical perspective, I always let the client introduce me to the appraisal conclusion and share their thoughts and emotions concerning them before we start a deeper conversation on areas of need. These areas are determined by the client, yet I find it helpful to keep in mind the hitherto undiscussed results. All areas of need should be touched upon and discussed, including why and how some results seem to be more important than others.

The higher the leadership level the more often **360° feedback** is used to help develop and improve leadership skills. In these anonymous feedbacks, the feedback providers are chosen by function. When chosen by the client, unfortunately, very often these feedbacks are not taken that seriously and lead to a "do-ut-des" situation. However, with proper 360° feedback, the target individual and feedback providers are trained in the process and return input on the coach's behaviour in a holistic way. This gives the individual the opportunity to examine themselves in the mirror of their co-workers' perceptions (Kwiatkowski, 2006, p. 161). The 360° tool offers a number of advantages, from increasing self-awareness and involving people at all levels of the organisation, to drawing attention to the leadership and cultural aspects of the organisation. Feedback can be taken on board by the individual in a considerate, mature and integrative way, but it can also be received negatively and cause harm, even trauma. Therefore, it is necessary for the coach to handle the results with a duty of care towards the client and their emotional reactions. Working with assessment tools can be boiled down to four basic questions: how attentively and carefully was it compiled, how does the client (emotionally) perceive the results, which areas of importance arise and need to be worked on, and what are the blind spots and real pain points which demand special attention and care?

Personality inventories

The most common inventories – Hogan, the Big Five, MBTI, DISC – are not assessment tools per se. They present a picture of how the individual sees themselves from the inside, and therefore allow an insight on self-perception. Whereas the MBTI and the DISC focus a little more on describing the personality type and less on personality development and improvement, Hogan and the Big Five usually depict personal strengths and weaknesses. All of these tests are completed through participant self-reporting, hence may present a self-ideal instead of a critical reflection of oneself. The quality of the results therefore depends on the honesty and openness of the participants.

Some of these inventories are rather demanding in their application and require intensive training and also licensing before they can be used. I would therefore recommend against trying to explain or understand results when not sufficiently trained in the use of these instruments – misinterpretations and misunderstanding can cause quite painful and irritable reactions on the client side, and this presents a huge risk of destroying an underdeveloped self-esteem. I also recommend reading the case study of Kwiatkowski (2006), in which he self-critically describes how he uses the MBTI together with 360° feedback in a coaching setting.

22

Working in and with the relationship – the coach as instrument

The most important element of psychodynamic coaching, and that which most clearly distinguishes it from other coaching approaches, is the use of oneself in the coaching relationship as an instrument in service of the client. By instrument I mean the idea of using the coach's own feelings, private and professional memory and physical body not only for cognitive insights and reflections, but as a basis for reception, for resonance, for associations, for emotional contagion, for personal transformation. Psychodynamic coaching assumes that all our reflections and insights as a coach are particularly emotionally influenced by the client and by our own past experiences. The work with and within the relationship is crucial, since most of the coaching themes concern relational patterns – whether they are unconscious, or visible and behavioural. Working with oneself, the own self, entails working with transference, countertransference and also projective identification. It can be best described as a way of participating in observation, in which the coach observes the client whilst simultaneously observing him-/herself as part of the situation. In other words, the coach has one foot in the situation and relationship and the other foot remains, at least temporarily, outside of the relationship. The art of the coach is to triangulate the situation and thus simultaneously become the observing third.

Transference and projections

Everybody, thus every client, acts and reacts according to prior interactional experiences, having formed over the course of their life a specific style of social interaction. Early feelings in particular are continuously repeated in relation to people in the present – colleagues, bosses, friends, partners, etc. The first target of transference in the coaching session is the coach. So, the client projects their expectations of social interaction onto the coach in behaving as if the coach were one of his or her caregivers or another important relationship. It is necessary to decipher this transference as being a part of the client and not as an aspect of the coach. Defensive reactions such as rejecting a proposition or hypothesis can be interpreted as the client seeing in the coach an authority figure, such as a parent, which precipitates an urge to resist. It is necessary for the coach to understand their own transference processes, especially their own public perception in contrast to self-perception. Consequently, the coach must not take the transference of the client to be the truth about themselves. When a coach is for example perceived as the grandiose know-it-all, to which the client reacts in admiration, this perception does not necessarily reflect reality, it could also be the outcome of the client projecting their narcissistic desire for grandiosity on to the coach. Thus, thorough training is necessary prior to working actively with transference, since one's public image is deeply connected with one's anxieties, desires, needs and hopes.

A practical instrument in this endeavour which provides a conceptual structure for transference is the "relationship-triangle", which uses three sides: the self, the present-other and the past-other to illustrate the effects of transference. Deconstructing conflict situations helps the client to understand how early feelings influence actual perceptions of the other (Kets de Vries & Engellau, 2010).

Countertransference

Countertransference is more complex. In understanding the otherness of the client, it is necessary to understand the other or the stranger in one's self. One's emotional reactions may simply represent one's personal reactions towards the other, a process which must be understood and worked through by the coach as part of a personal learning process. However, it could also indicate how the client feels without knowing that they feel this way – it can represent a split-off emotion or emotional situation, which the coach then feels also. For example, the coach may feel a sudden deep anxiety while the client is talking and might than realise that this anxiety does not relate to the emotions they would experience if they were in the client's position. This experience of feeling another's anxiety as if it were one's own is a very important diagnostic tool for the coach. When experiencing such a situation, it is rarely helpful to immediately address it with the client – more appropriate would be for the coach to first better understand their emotional reaction and develop more in-depth insights into the client's emotional reactions through allowing them to describe, symbolically or metaphorically, or even draw, their experiences. Thus, the unconscious dynamic will present itself differently and will therefore be more accessible for the client.

Projective identification

This mechanism can kick in in both the client and the coach and is an important contribution to change in clients.

> First, there is the fantasy of projecting a part of oneself into another person and of that part taking over the person from within, then there is pressure exerted via the interpersonal interaction such as the "recipient" of the projection experiences pressure to think, feel and behave in a manner congruent with the projection; finally the projected feelings, after being "psychologically processed" by the recipient, are re-internalized by the projector.
>
> (Odgen, 1979, p. 358)

This means that it is necessary for the coach to observe their own inner-reactions to find out whether they are their own or whether they can be identified as different from their "normal" reactions and then check and adapt the reaction in order to psychologically process it. Of course, this is not always possible; as reactions can become infected by this process without the coach realising it, the coach has then become part of the game. However, when later self-reflecting on reactions and using supervision to support this self-reflection, it will become possible for the coach to understand why and how they reacted, recognise their inner-hook and learn how to process the client's feelings differently next time.

Using oneself as an instrument sounds very dry and at the same time very complex – which it is. Creating awareness, insights and change in a client is difficult, and changing oneself is the most difficult task for both the client and the coach. The coach also undergoes personal development and change in this continuous process of observation, reflection, empathic feelings, contagious emotions, differentiations and dissections, psychological digestion and post-session reflections. This is the nature of the job.

23

Working at the core of the client's question

Clients usually have a specific question and a corresponding problem which they want to discuss and solve, but very often psychodynamic coaching reveals a different question underneath the surface. I have had clients who were experiencing difficulty in their leadership role and subject to complaint from their subordinates, female clients who were finding it difficult to deal with a male (macho) culture, male clients who felt that their performance problems were somehow linked with their leadership but did not know how to solve them, team clients who were unable to effectively manage their meetings, and clients who required support and discourse whilst going through a change process within their company, a role change or a personal change affecting their professional life, to name just a few. These problems interfere with personal and organisational performance and induce a learning and development process on a personal level. Some leaders also seek coaching to improve their overall performance and/or to work on their leadership behaviour generally. These people understand that without honest and clear feedback, which colleagues and subordinates rarely dare to contribute, only limited enhancement of their leadership capabilities and leadership performance will be possible.

Whether the client brings a clear question or a less specific development need, the coaching process follows the classical approach of most consulting endeavours. After an initial diagnostic and analytic phase, which is part of the intervention, work on the core question(s) begins and gradually digs deeper, either through prior development of a concept (which is rather unusual in psychodynamic coaching) or by delving further into the subject matter so that new insights develop and behavioural and cognitive changes are discussed and applied. These will later be evaluated before entering into a finalising phase to seclude and end the coaching process.

Classical approaches within the relationship

After the opening diagnostic phase (see Chapter 20), in the next phase of conceptualising and working on the core subject the coach focusses even more on the use of unusual words, stories, explanations, situations as images or symbols of the unconscious, and conscious emotional aspects of the client's situation and question. **ORA and the six domains** provide a methodological frame for this. Others use **symbolic expressions** directly as an aid to explaining what is going on in the client's inner-world (see Chapter 24). In psychodynamic coaching, the **coach uses him-/herself as an instrument** to develop a deeper understanding of emotions and emotional reactions (see Chapter 22).

The Socratic dialogue

A more cognitive approach is the **Socratic dialogue**. This is a specific method of leading a discourse with the client, asking questions, and developing and checking assumptions of both the client and the coach. The Socratic dialogue stemming from philosophy was understood by Socrates and Plato as a means of "healing the soul". It is worth noting, however, that during their era psychology and philosophy were still considered as one. In modern times, cognitive therapy has integrated the Socratic dialogue in its therapeutic reservoir, but I also find it extremely useful from a psychodynamic perspective – the reflective attitude of the coach being the medium for the projective aspects can be applied whilst using the method as a way of approaching the client's thoughts and feelings.

The Socratic dialogue is a conversational style based on a not-knowing, explorative, naïve questioning and an understanding, interested attitude which adopts curiosity and humility. It supports the client in reflecting their own way of thinking in discovering (destructive) assumptions and belief systems, inconsistencies and biases so that they can develop new insights and reactions (Stavemann, 2002, p. 4). At the same time, it helps establish a collaborative relationship, conveys empathy and contributes to a process of guided discovery. It consists mainly of systematic questioning, inductive reasoning, and discovering causal irrational attributions and reasoning to facilitate a change of perspective and explore alternative reasoning with different emotional and behavioural reactions.

The following dialogue example gives a simplified overview of how this method works across five phases or steps. In psychodynamic coaching, one would focus more on the exploration of a feeling, whereas in cognitive approaches the focus lies on the belief or thought as the entry point.

1 Elicit the belief/thought/feeling – assessment of the question

Coach: You have said that you always have difficulties with Mr. X (Mr. X is the chairman of the supervisory board where the client is the CEO). How do you feel when you think of the last time you met Mr. X?

Client: I feel like a little boy when he asks me to report the numbers to him.

2 Link the feeling with a behaviour

C: And how do you react when you feel like a little boy?

Cl: Hmmm. . . . I get numb . . . don't know what to say and withdraw from the conversation.

C: What does "feeling like a little boy" mean to you?

Cl: When I was a little boy, my parents always told me that I am not good for anything and that they have to make sure that I do things right by controlling what I am doing.

C: Do you remember a specific situation?

Cl: Well, I remember once, when I had to go and buy cigarettes for my father, I got distracted on the way and bought the wrong brand. My father got angry, told me off and wrote the right brand name down in big letters on a piece of paper and gave it to me to make me feel ashamed and to make sure I remembered next time.

3 Connect the feeling-thought-behaviour sequence with an empathic response

C: This sounds very painful for a little boy. It must be difficult to have those same feelings now; maybe you feel incapable and worthless in these situations? What does it mean to feel that somebody has to control what you do to make sure it happens?

Cl: I get angry and want to shout at the person. I want to tell them that I know what I am doing and that I do not need any kind of control.

4 Inductive questioning

C: Do you always get angry when somebody wants to discuss or understand the results of the work with you? When one of your team members ask you, for example?

Cl: No, when a team member asks me, it feels different, I feel that I am responsible for explaining, teaching and somewhat educating the person.

C: And when your friend asks you to explain, for example, how you cut your roses, how do you feel then?

Cl: Well, I feel proud and as an expert, because my roses are superb and I am happy to explain my understanding.

5 Eliminative Causal Reasoning

C: So, when you feel you are seen as the expert you like to explain and do not feel controlled?

Cl: Yes, I even enjoy talking about my achievements and like to share them with others to help them get better at what they are doing.

C: But when somebody in an authoritative position asks you, you feel controlled, right?

Cl: Yes. Then I sink back in time and feel as if my father were standing next to me, I feel helpless and want to shout at him, which of course I do not dare to do.

C: How could you transfer the feeling you have as an expert to the situation with the chairman? What would the chairman have to do?

Cl: See me as an expert, then it would be easier.

C: So, do you need to be seen as an expert to feel like an expert?

Cl: Hmmm. . . . Well. . . . No, I guess I need to see myself as the expert, independent of the other person's opinion.

C: So, what could be your next step in the conversation with your chairman?

Cl: I could remember that I am the expert and explain what has happened. I would just need to change perspective.

Of course, this is a very basic example that simply serves to demonstrate aspects of the Socratic method. Oberholser (e.g. 1993) provides a systematic overview and, although he is concerned with therapy, the method itself can be applied in psychodynamic coaching as one intervention or in combination with other techniques.

24

Dealing with emotions

Relationship is key in the psychodynamic coaching process. In all relationships, emotions play the pivotal role, hence the coach must understand how to deal with emotions from a psychodynamic perspective. By "dealing with emotions" I do not refer to how to discern them, that has already been discussed, rather, I mean what to do with them professionally once they are in the room. What do you do with an anxious or frightened client, with anger, with frustration, with sadness, and also with delight and over-excitement?

Show empathy

When a client presents a difficult emotion, it is the task of the coach to react appropriately by demonstrating **empathic understanding** of the emotion and also that it has a reason to exist in the here and now and will be dealt with respectfully and seriously. Yet this does not imply reacting as if the client were a good friend – it is not appropriate from a professional stance to console, embrace or touch a client experiencing sorrow or other difficult emotions. Furthermore, as a coach you must never criticize, devalue, underestimate, play down or question the client or the emotion itself.

Approaching a first understanding also includes **recognising the emotion** by naming or labelling it so that it can be talked about openly. Once an unclear and difficult emotional state is given a name it has already lost some of its destructive power as it becomes all too human. Part of this recognition process is to normalise these seemingly irrational aspects so that they can be observed and studied. This not only helps the client to overcome the shame often accompanying strong (negative) emotional reactions, but also has a relieving effect, similar to as if a large weight has been cast off. Freud compared this effect of the talking cure with a confession – daring to name an until so far un-nameable emotion has a similar effect.

Further explore

As a next step it can be helpful to **explore the emotion** itself, the situation and the context in which it develops to foster a deeper understanding for the client by asking good and profound questions. Good questions in this instance would be respectful, open, **naïvely curious**, interested and considerate of the client. They are not unveiling or investigative but follow an explorative path with genuine interest.

Interpret

Having developed a first understanding, the coach may also have created an initial hypothesis regarding the history, appearance and pain points that cause the specific emotional reaction. At this point, the coach can begin to **connect it** with other reactions in similar settings in the present, with their own observations of the client's reactions, and with past experiences of the client so that pattern-like aspects become accessible.

For both the client and the coach, this exploration involves a process that **oscillates** between **diving** into the emotion, be it pleasant or painful, going alongside it and taking up **a meta-position** for purposes of reflection, observation and reasoning. This meta-position also helps to illuminate the reason behind it and the former, presumably protective, **purpose** of the emotional or behavioural reaction. Most strong emotional or behavioural reactions are linked to painful and unpleasant past experiences and have a defensive or signalling function.

Resources, the transitional space and a larger emotional repertoire

Experiencing strong emotions and behavioural patterns is unusual and can be very stressful. To achieve insight and change it is helpful to create a transitional space (see Chapter 17) that provides the client with the opportunity to play with and step outside their usual habits and emotional prisons. With playfulness and creativity, the coach can create opportunities for them to re-invent themselves and to create awareness that they do have different options. This entails the capacity of the coach to look for resources in the client, see opportunities instead of threats through **positive reframing**, encouraging new behaviours and reactions, and even rehearsing these new ways and creating "a safe and empathic identity laboratory" (Kets de Vries & Engellau, 2010, p. 214) for the client. The role of the coach is to allow the client to experiment and to create a holding and containing environment as a means of working with defences, anxieties and ambivalences, whilst simultaneously being empathic, explorative, non-judgemental, open, flexible and not-knowing. Allowing sufficient time for new insights and meanings to emerge within the relationship may prove contrary to what was assumed at the beginning of the work, but is extremely helpful. This can elicit further acceptance by the client and help them deal with future situations that cause the emotion to arise. The next step is to then **develop a solution** in the sense that alternative perspectives on the situation and possible alternative reactions – scenarios of what could be avoided or managed differently – can be discussed, thought through, explored and even trained and rehearsed. Black and white reactions will be opened up to an array of new possible reactions that form the grey area in between – **enlarging the emotional and behavioural repertoire** is the final goal.

25

Using symbols

Accessing the unconscious entails working with aspects such as fantasies, dreams and creativity. Since these elements often reveal new insights, here we will explain how to work with them.

Symbols are the starting point; they are, according to Jung, the language of the unconscious and of the soul. Symbols as well as images transport unconscious material, emotions, memories of experiences and events, insights, conflicts and other psychic content. As an unconscious creation of and a solution for a conscious problem, they can serve as a vehicle for psychological diagnosis (Roth, 2003) due to the fact that they can also reflect difficulties and central queries. Working with symbols facilitates new insights into difficult work or life situations and basic personal issues and contributes to personal development by providing new and different perspectives.

Almost everything can have a **symbolic meaning**, be seen or understood as a symbol or can be used as a symbol in a coaching context. We can differentiate between inner-symbols such as dreams, fantasies, specific words, own preferences, habits, gestures, own creations (writings, drawings, etc.), and outer-symbols which stem from society, culture, religion and art, such as myths and fairy tales, paintings, sculptures, plays, lyrics, objects of desire, of collection, of phantasy, etc.

Both inner- and outer-symbols can be brought by the client or identified by the coach and used to initiate exploration of their symbolic meaning. This might make sense when a specific word or gesture frequently creates irritation, a (day)dream appears in an important decision-making situation, a sudden idea, memory or object coming to mind in a difficult situation makes one recall unthought aspects, or e.g. a specific colour creates curiosity or refusal. Anything which creates some kind of attraction or rejection in the client's professional or personal life which the client thinks about or talks about in the session can be used to gain a deeper understanding of the inner-world in connection with the respective outer-context. The main character of a symbol is its complex, multilayered, infinite meaning and dimensions of interpretation – it is not a clear sign or a precise equation, it is blurry, mysterious, unclear, and can only be explored intuitively – and although the key is the individual attributed connotation, cultural knowledge of the background, use or history of the symbol can support and amplify the exploration to gain additional insight.

There are three entry points into working with symbolic meaning:

- The client can describe an important dream, daydream or phantasy which they feel to be of significance
- An important present or past situation can be used as a starting point
- The client can be asked to, for example, draw or paint the feeling, the situation or aspects of the content that is bothering them

For most clients this approach is new and unusual, and they may feel embarrassed to, for example, draw their emotions, and use the excuse that they cannot draw or paint. Therefore, the most important prerequisite is openness, emotional and intellectual curiosity and willingness as well as a familiarity with the use of symbols on the part of the coach in regard to the client's inner-world and essence.

When working with symbols, a number of techniques can be employed. These will be summarised in Figure 25.1.

This does not represent a linear but a multi-step process that moves backwards and forward until an "a-ha" moment has been reached with the client.

The coach either begins the process by initiating exploration of an important moment, gesture, object, dream, etc. that the client feels to be of ineffable importance, or a certain aspect of the work they themselves are drawn to, symbolically.

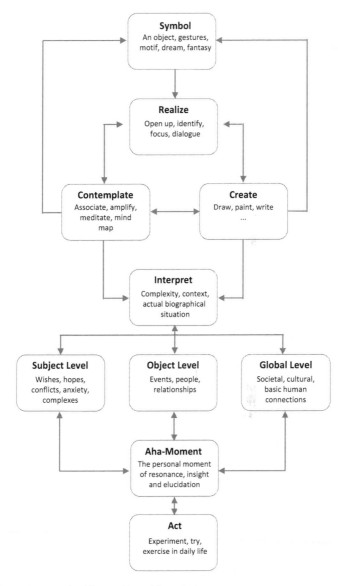

Figure 25.1 Method for working with symbols

Source: Adapted from Müller & Knoll (1998, p. 223)

The first step is to **realise** this subject of significance as a symbol, to focus on it, and create space for reflecting, perceiving, feeling and diving into it; one can even enter into a dialogue with the symbol by e.g. imagining that it is a dialogue partner.

Contemplating then means to free associate what comes to mind, to centre the attention around the associations and around the symbol and amplify it by placing the symbol in a broader human context; one can meditate about it or draw a mind-map of the various associations and connotations.

The client can then be asked or may even suggests **to create** their own image of the symbol using a pen or colours. This creative representation allows for a very individual access to the more unconscious meanings of the symbol. For me it is always a first moment of a-ha when I see how a client perceives this subject of significance from a symbolic perspective. Many questions, clarifications and stories can be designed around such a drawing or painting. This creative image might also represent the actual problem from a different and more playful perspective that includes the resources and the solution to overcoming it. Contemplation and further creation can be a process in its own right.

After spending a moment with the complex, paradoxical and multidimensional nature of the symbol, **interpretation** commences with exploring first ideas or insights that may connect the symbol with the actual life situation, such as memories and feelings and, in the biographical context, experiences, similarities, analogies and other life situations. One can then progress to exploring the **subject level** further in reflecting upon which inner-aspects of the personality structure are represented in the symbol. In dream interpretation this is one possible means of understanding the appearing figures as inner personality components. This raises the question of what they represent in the sense of one's relationship to oneself, to conflict, to unknown aspects and to negative or positive emotions connected with them. It might also point to creative resources and hidden competencies, life enhancing and enriching perspectives, and possible routes out of the client's own inner-prison.

By observing the **object level**, one can understand the nature of outer relationships, since the object level perspective connects the symbol to real people in the actual life situation. On the **global level**, the symbol can be explored regarding its archetypal and cultural meaning – with existential questions about life, death, love, self-awareness, individuation, spirituality, etc. Here it can be helpful to use anthropological, theological or mythological literature as well as etymological encyclopaedias.

This process of working with the symbolic meaning of the subject of significance will at best lead to the moment of a-ha – which starts with a feeling of inner-resonance and develops into a deeply felt (and maybe not yet completely intellectually understood) new insight and elucidation. The emotional feeling of this a-ha moment is more important than a complete rational understanding. Only over time and reflection will a symbol give away its deeper meaning. Eventually the insight can be integrated into real life and daily routine through experimentation with this new perspective, new behaviours and new thinking and feeling routines. One has to allow time for this transference process – old routines are akin to highways in the mind. A new highway does not suddenly appear; it evolves from a dirt track, to a road and so on.

26

Coaching female leaders

Is coaching a woman different from coaching a man? Yes and no. Male executives still dominate top management positions – in number and in behaviour. One must admit that even after more than 100 years of fighting for equal rights, women still do not have equal influence or role in economic organisations. Male standards of communication and leadership dictate the terms through which women must negotiate to find their way to the top. We live in a world where gender biases and stereotypes prevail in the corporate environment.

I have made a number of observations on this point when coaching women:

- Women feel they are not recognised in terms of their personal job contribution, often other criteria seem to be more important
- Women are criticised for daring to want it all and at the same time (work and family and friends)
- Women feel that they are not supposed to aspire to top management positions
- Women feel that they are not supposed to want to be in power or enjoy it

Stereotypes, biases, role expectations

Stereotypes such as that which implies men are better leaders still unconsciously dominate our thinking. The IAT (Implicit Association Test) has been developed to determine how stereotypes influence us beyond our cognitive perception and has proven that although only 26% of men and 17% of women believe that men are better leaders, 64% (men) and 49% (women) implicitly adhere to this stereotype

(Diverseo, 2012). Basic role expectations are also attributed very differently. For men, these expectations revolve around **agency** (being assertive, self-reliant, tough, autonomous and self-promoting – which creates authority figure, leader and "breadwinner" roles), whereas women still pivot on **community** (being close to others, connecting with family and friends, cooperating and taking care of others, maintaining harmony, being empathic, helpful or nurturing – which leads to traditionally feminine roles as caretakers) (Valerio, 2009). Unfortunately, these role expectations induce resistance to female leadership, specific double bind and double standard problems for women, and their competence being questioned. By "double bind" I refer to the impasse faced by most women: when they take agency, they are easily seen as being too tough, too assertive, too aggressive or strident – whereas when they focus on communal behaviour they are seen as too nice or too soft, not tough enough (Valerio, 2009).

A number of further biases during selection procedures result in men favouring a male for a task as they consider it to be a simpler solution.

The following biases come into play:

- *Mirror-image error:* the tendency to use oneself as a starting point: "I am good so the other has to be like me" (recruiting in one's own image)
- *Central tendency:* the tendency to choose the mean value rather than the extremes (recruiting a woman often needs more explanation)
- *Logical error:* the tendency to link two unconnected aspects in judgement as if they were logically connected (appearance and performance, rhetoric and abstract thinking)
- *Halo effect:* the tendency to assume that a person who performs well or badly in one area, also performs well or badly in other areas

Women may also be on the receiving end of specific projections which can have further distorting or damaging effects. These projections stem from male experiences with their mothers, grandmothers and sisters and can be manifold (Eden, 2006).

Coaching aspects

To summarise, most women in their job environment occupy a distinct emotional and factual position to their male counterparts. Those undergoing coaching may want to find their own way of managing these expectations, biases and male-dominated organisational cultures to achieve and fulfil their own job ideals and needs. A number of rules can help them (and the coach) find a path through the jungle:

- Question your own role prejudices (coach and client) which might stand in the way of a more fulfilling job (perception)
- Get some distance on the situation from a play perspective, different actors having different goals and aims
- Don't take devaluing or aggressive behaviour from males as a personal attack, develop the capacity to split off emotional attacks instead of taking them in
- Remember that everything comes at a price and everybody must make choices, regardless of gender
- There is always the possibility of leaving the organisation for a more suitable job environment

Coaching in this sense has the aim of enabling women to develop self-awareness of their own competencies and capabilities, to connect them with their wishes and hopes and align them with the outer-reality and real situation of the organisation.

This knowledge of stereotypes and biases can help in working with male clients who have difficulties in promoting women, working with a specific woman or working under a female leader for the first time.

27

Understanding and addressing the context

The continuous presence of the organisation for which the client works provides an explicit and implicit external context and distinguishes psychodynamic coaching from psychotherapy and coaching in the following areas:

Threefold listening

As a third party, the organisation can be present either as an external reality, to be engaged with or not, or as an internal reality in the mind of the client and the coach. For the coach, this means keeping the third party in mind throughout. In this **"threefold listening"** mode the coach must be attentive to the individual, to the representation of the organisation in the client's mind and to the reality of the organisation beyond the client. This listening mode surfaces the client's dilemmas, difficulties and challenges – transference and countertransference deliver important information in this regard. Whatever the client brings to the consulting room can be read both personally and organisationally, and implicates keeping in mind a complex network of influencing components (see Figure 27.1).

In the middle axis we find the connection between person and role, including the notion of self-esteem as another linking component between personal development and organisational constraints – the organisation in the mind is an interplay of these aspects within the person's psyche.

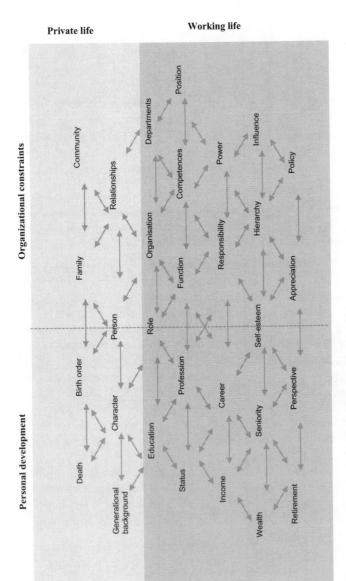

Figure 27.1 The contextual framework for executive coaching

Source: Further developed and cited after Huffington (2006, p. 46)

Finding, making and taking an organisational role – ORA

This axis directs us to the ORA approach (see Chapter 3). The development of the executive role is based on the three steps of **finding**, **making** and **taking the role** – from a personal perspective within the organisation. A role is an idea in the mind which is dynamic, not fixed. The way a person takes on a role is influenced by how the individual perceives the organisation and its aim, the personal desire regarding the perceived aim, by the way the individual takes ownership of the role and by the actions the individual takes to fulfil their own aims as well as those of the organisation (Reed & Bazalgette, 2006).

Finding the role in the context of coaching involves listening to the different role aspects the client describes in order to decipher the subjective mental construct and create a meaning around it. This helps the client to develop an understanding of the organisation as the third party in the room as well as a contextual system so that present and future behaviours and actions can be reflected upon using this framework. The next step is **making the role**, which incorporates the realisation of constraints and boundaries and further outer pressures resulting from other person–role–systems. This requires reflection on the functioning of the system and the cause and effect relationships regarding the client as an individual, and beyond. This enables the client to take initiatives on behalf of the organisation as a system. Step three, **taking the role**, involves experimenting with the hypothesis developed over the course of the coaching, and learning and adapting behaviours, reflections and emotional reactions that take place in the organisational reality.

Managing the triangular relationship

If the client is the organisation and not the individual, the coach must exercise additional care in managing this triangular relationship between themselves, the organisation as the client and the individual as the "end client". To this end the threefold listening mode gains more importance. The challenges this presents for the coach beyond the contracting phase are manifold:

- Working in a triangular setting entails **the risk of splitting** into parties of two against the third. The coach must be aware of any attempts by either party to draw him/her onto "their side" to argue or fight against the other. In some cases, coaches can be instrumentalised for the sake of the organisation to educate a non-willing employee for its own purpose.
- **Conscious conflict** between the diverging needs and aims of the organisation and the individual client are another danger. The coach and client as the individual must carefully consider and discuss what course of action to take if this happens. Ultimately the individual client can only contribute to organisational performance based on their own willingness to do so. If the conflict is unsolvable, leaving the organisation may be the only option.
- Working with the organisation is represented by how the coach provides **feedback to the organisation** about the individual, and to the organisation about itself. A third way of working with the organisation comes into being when coaching the C-suite, who have the power and the means to influence the whole organisation.

Further contexts

What we have discussed above regarding the organisation can also be applied to the working group as context for individual coaching.

Appropriate attention is needed for the **societal context** in which the coaching takes place. Cultural, language and gender aspects can affect the organisation in the mind as well as in role perception. Cultural and language connotations as well as stereotypes that stem from the meeting of different nationalities in the work group, in the organisation or only for the individual working in a foreign context, can lead to severe misinterpretations and mis-matched emotional or behavioural reactions. The coach must be sensitive to these cultural and gender aspects and be prepared to question their own culturally influenced perceptions as well as work with the client on these unconscious pre-judgements and inherent value systems.

28

Coaching teams in organisations

Coaching a group differs from coaching an individual. Working with a group or a team is more demanding for the coach since each individual brings their own personal story and interests, and as the group or team itself has a story and an aim; collusions within the group as well as collusions with other groups within the organisation are possible, and many transferences and counter-transferences can be picked up. Since we are in the area of executive coaching, we prioritise (top) management team coaching, which is more relevant on the leadership level. The difference between a **group and a team** can best be described by the famous oath of Alexandre Dumas's Three Musketeers: "One for all and all for one". Reciprocity and interpersonal trust are the key ingredients which differentiate a group and a team (Kets de Vries, 2011). We also assume here that team coaching takes place within one organisation and not across several organisations. (For cross-organisational teams see Schruijer, Vansina, 2008).

Issues and aims

Team coaching has a partly facilitating character in that it helps to find a solution to a problem but goes beyond this in the sense that the psychodynamic team coach works with and within the team dynamics, shares openly their observations and hypotheses about the functioning and the performance of the group and in certain phases keeps the dialogue open and unmanaged. The basic idea – just as in individual coaching – is to **improve the collective performance** of the team as well as the performance of **the individual** within the team. Different team types (stable teams, "cabin crew teams", standing project teams, evolutionary teams, virtual teams; see Clutterbuck,

2014) each demand that the coach adopt a specific mindset and understanding of their functioning. It is therefore extremely important to clarify the goal of the team coaching before it commences. From a psychodynamic stance it would be best to involve the whole team in this coaching goal definition process, which itself becomes the first team coaching intervention.

The aim of the psychodynamic team coach is to facilitate awareness of unconscious team dynamics and their emotional undercurrents. This is achieved by overcoming defences, solving underlying issues and helping develop emotional flexibility and the capacity for dialogue and shared reflection so that the team can solve future issues unaided.

Team coaching is often considered when dysfunctional group dynamics prevail (Kets de Vries, 2011), for example:

- Interpersonal dynamics: conflicts, emotional difficulties, developing emotional intelligence
- Temporal issues: how the team manages and emphasises the past, present and future
- Managing key processes: goal setting and management, functional analysis, innovation, decision-making and communication
(Clutterbuck, 2014, p. 274)

The overarching aims are to foster cooperation and collaboration, and through this a climate of openness, honesty and trust in the final goal can be achieved, improving individual and team performance.

Working with the team

The **opening** session may bring together all group members to discuss the team coaching goals. Another approach is to interview each member of the team individually and collect their ideas and perspectives on the subject matter. Thus, the coach can develop a basic impression of the individual personalities that comprise the team. Team heads that participate in the coaching process generally request that this step is taken at the onset – it helps to reduce the anxiety a completely open process would create. The **diagnostic** interview round allows the coach to develop first insights and hypotheses, which are then shared and discussed with the whole group. These interviews are already part of the team coaching intervention.

Confidentiality and boundaries are issues for the whole team. When the team head is part of the team coaching process, confidentiality regarding individual issues or individual performance can be threatened. If possible, these boundaries should be clarified before the coaching commences. It is likely that this will be an ongoing subject of discussion since team members are often afraid to share their personal perceptions, perspectives and ideas for fear of losing face, reputation or the image they have created for themselves. Since openness, honesty and trust are a major goal, the coaching will focus on enabling the team members to more openly share their personal emotional and intellectual contributions, as well as the anxieties involved in doing so.

Several interventions support an open dialogue:

- Sitting in a circle, without tables, computers, mobiles, etc.
- Starting off the session with each team member sharing what they have emotionally experienced on the way to the meeting
- Sharing aspects of their personal history by answering basic questions about personal details such as their hometown, hobbies, first job, worst job, number of siblings, etc.
- Sharing personal stories by either presenting themselves through a self-portrait as, e.g. the animal they would like to be, by sharing their personal life-story, by sharing special events such as the moment they chose their career path, their most beautiful/difficult experience, etc.
- Sharing assessment results (360°) or taking a personality test together and sharing the results (e.g. MBTI)
- Identifying their single most important contribution to the team and the area that they must work on for the good of the team, starting with the team leader

These exercises create the grounds for **courageous conversations**, which means to engage in a dialogue with "people we don't normally talk to about things we normally don't talk about" (Kets de Vries, 2011). These courageous conversations are the result of as well as the grounds for continuous openness and honesty. Lencioni (2002) identified five **dysfunctions** which must be overcome if team work is to be effective: absence of trust, fear of conflict, lack of commitment, avoidance of accountability and inattention to results. His framework can be helpful in devising a team coaching approach for a dysfunctional team that is under pressure to perform. From a psychodynamic perspective I would add two more dysfunctions: lack of self-reflection on the individual level, likewise on the team level. The latter includes reflection on system aspects by looking at intergroup relations within and even across the organisation. Regular, positively framed **open reflection** on what has been learnt helps to ensure long-term success as well as identify further areas that would benefit from improvement.

Team coaching can be integrated into regular meetings, can take place during designated time slots within a regular meeting or be conducted on its own. One can also start with special team coaching days which can over time be gradually phased out and integrated into the regular meetings.

Coaching a (leadership) team always bears the risk that the coach develops an unconscious collusion with the group's main issue – especially when over a longer coaching process relationships between the team and the team coach develop and individuals begin to get to know each other well on a personal level. The temptation for the coach here is to not only to become part of the team or organisation, but also to step into the leader's role in a weakness of leadership. Other pitfalls for the coach are the risk of becoming subverted into existing group norms or to enter into a situation of dependency whereby the team expects the coach to solve their problems (Clutterbuck, 2014). All these situations can be integrated into the work with the team through self-reflection on the part of the coach, supported by supervision, and the coach sharing these insights with the team.

Depending on the issues facing the team, individual coaching sessions and reflections can be added as further components with the special safeguard of confidentiality for the coach. Privacy boundaries can be easily broken in a setting where the team coach also coaches the members individually, and as such demands greater care, attention and delicacy. When the team coach simultaneously works with the group, with the individual, and with the individual as part of the group, this is a highly demanding balancing act of collective and individual work.

ENDING THE COACHING

Every coaching relationship is a time-limited endeavour, whether the exact number of sessions is predetermined, or progress is open-ended. There must come a time when coach and client agree that the work is over: either because the main question has been worked through in a way that enables the client to continue unaided, as a result of budget restrictions, because the situation has changed or – rarely, but also possible – the relationship between coach and client has taken a negative course.

29

Ending the coaching relationship

Preparing the ending

The task of the coach is to **prepare a final review process** – first inviting the client to review the experience, the goal, the achievements, important insights, moments of despair and happiness and changes in feelings over time – if they want to. Second, the coach must carefully prepare for this review process by reflecting on their notes, their starting hypothesis, the development of the relationship and the client, and on their own feelings during this process and at the end of the relationship. In the review conversation the client should start to share their perspective, which the coach can then react to, expand on or contribute an alternative perspective (Sanders, 2011). A good closure will **celebrate the successes** and share the positive emotions around achievements, yet it will also **share moments of disappointment**, anger and other shortcomings. As many feelings as possible shall be verbalised so that no loose ends remain in the room.

If the **client is the organisation**, then the first task is to prepare and go over the review process with the client, reflect on the coaching objectives and achievements, and then reflect on and agree on what to share with the representative of the organisation. The individual client should prepare examples of what has changed and how one could observe these changes in behaviour. Ultimately it is the individual client who should describe how they have benefited from the coaching process. If necessary, further development issues can be discussed.

Objectives, definitions of success and performance perceptions can change over time, and the client, coach and organisation's perspectives on such may differ. The coach must therefore be capable of balancing these diverging opinions and holding conflicting tensions in mind, while at the same time respecting the disparate interests and addressing them in the setting that they belong to. If possible, this should be openly integrated into the end process, but not every personal achievement of the client needs to be shared with the organisational representative.

Emotions at the end of a relationship

At the conclusion of the relationship, many different emotional states can be present. Even if the coaching was very successful, the end of a relationship is often not positively connotated. Throughout an intense relationship in which the client shares their vulnerabilities and the coach is emotionally involved, feelings of loss, sadness and mourning emerge. These feelings are a natural part of the process and shall be integrated and reflected on in the final sessions.

Premature endings are mostly unpleasant and can occur for many reasons: funding may suddenly be withdrawn, the client may reject the coaching or the coach or gradually drop out. An early ending poses a dual challenge for the coach: the coach must terminate (if possible) this coaching relationship with the same level of due care and professionalism as when concluding a successful one. On the other hand, the coach must also **deal with their own emotions** associated with loss, but also with failure, such as anger, self-doubt, shame, confusion and irritation. An early ending presents an important learning experience for the coach – when they are capable, honest and self-aware enough to recognise their own mistakes, misjudgements and misbehaviours. At the same time, it is also important for the coach to understand which factors were beyond their control during the coaching process (Sandler, 2011).

Other feelings at the end can centre around **dependency**. A healthy dependency is a natural aspect of a personal development process, whereby the client not only opens up emotionally but also, in difficult moments of inner-confusion and irritation, depends on the coach and their judgement, containment and attachment (Sandler, 2011).

The goal for the client is to develop their **own inner-coach**, which over the course of time will take over and provide a self-sustainable affirming, guiding and supporting role and lead to autonomy and independence. Obviously, too strong an attachment or dependency needs to be verbalised, discussed and made part of the developmental process. Yet attachments and dependencies can also be of a temporary nature and offer an important insight for the client.

30

Training, ethics and elements of good practice

Coaching is not a universal cure-all, and psychodynamic coaching even less so. Nor is the psychodynamic approach suitable for every coach (and client). Thorough psychological and psychodynamic theoretical knowledge is necessary, as well as practical training, experience, supervision and a willingness to constantly reflect on one's own practice. Some coaches prefer more pragmatic, solution-oriented techniques, more cognitive approaches or the application of concrete business experience and their own convictions and beliefs. The constant questioning, reflection and self-reflection seem to be especially difficult for former long-term managers who want to develop into the coaching profession, where their action and solution-oriented attitude may serve as an obstacle.

Deduced from many studies on the **effectiveness** of psychodynamic therapy in comparison with other therapies (Roberts & Jarrett, 2006) and extended to psychodynamic coaching, success depends on:

- The quality of the relationship between coach and client and how safe and well-understood the client feels
- The degree to which the coach can draw on a wide range of perceptions and interventions rather than rigidly adhering to a narrow framework
- The quality of the interventions, in the sense that they are offered cautiously, creatively and throughout a continual process of reflection and exchange

(Leuzinger-Bohleber, Stuhr, Rüger, & Beutel, 2003)

These elements foster the inner developmental process and help the client develop "the inner-coach" that will enable them to support themselves once the coaching has ended.

The requirements of good coaching

Thorough practical and theoretical psychodynamic and coaching training on an ongoing basis is necessary for the delivery of good coaching practice, and involves:

- Effective establishment of the coaching relationship
- Genuine commitment of the coach to the client and their success
- Clear contracting
- Honesty on the part of both the coach and the client organisation, with no secret agendas
- Appropriate task boundaries (not all issues that emerge need to be tackled)
- Appropriate role boundaries (for the coach)
- Effective promotion of growth for the client
- Awareness of the potential of the coach to create dependency in the client
- Awareness of own limitations on the part of the coach (self-reflection and self-management)
- A broad and flexible repertoire of interventions and methods of thinking and perceiving organisations and situations
- Regular review of one's work under formal and informal supervision

(Roberts & Jarrett, 2006)

Ethical requirements

The importance of adhering to basic ethical standards should be self-evident; nevertheless, the professional coaching federations (ICF, IAC, EMCC, AC, APECS and others) have developed codes of conduct and ethical ground rules to clarify their positions. Most of these federations apply similar ethical demands:

- Do no harm to the client (or to yourself)
- Do not exploit your position of power and status as a coach
- Avoid conflicts of interest; if they occur, be transparent and clarify roles and boundaries
- Maintain and manage confidences and boundaries
- Respect the client, the interests of the client and (of course) the law
- Do not knowingly lie to the client
- Do not cross boundaries between the professional and the personal (especially in dual or multiple relationships)
- Do not become sexually involved with the client

(Brennan & Wildflower, 2014, p. 430)

The following are factors in **bad or unethical coaching** practice:

- Losing sight of the client's interests or putting one's own interests first:
  - Inadequate self-reflection/self-management and a failure to admit mistakes or correct unhelpful behaviour
  - Clinging to one's own perspectives, values, stereotypes and biases without self-questioning
  - Failure to refer a client to a more suitable coach or psychotherapist when necessary
  - Retaining a client out of financial interest or out of fear of losing the client when there is no need for the coaching to continue

- Allowing the coaching to become instrumentalised by the organisation for their own purpose
- Working without thorough training and supervision, especially in opening up the psychic "Pandora's Box" when working with clients who are not suitably prepared
- Misrepresenting one's own abilities to deliver an outcome as a means of keeping or reassuring the client

- Becoming emotionally involved in the client's issues and indirectly or inadvertently manipulating the client for one's own needs

(Brenann & Wildflower, 2014)

One final remark: as there is no established quality assurance for or formal qualification associated with the title "psychodynamic coach", adhering to the ethical standards of the professional coaching federations would exclude a misuse of this title and request honesty and transparency regarding background and experience. The fundamental question of how much psychodynamic training is necessary before one can use the title remains to be answered. This book aims to provide an overview of the most important theoretical and practical elements. Theory, however, cannot replace the most important ingredients of the psychodynamic approach: continuous reflection on the work with the client and on oneself with the utmost honesty and willingness to improve with every client and with every hour of coaching.

Bibliography

Allen, J. G., Fonagy, P., & Bateman, A. (2008). *Mentalizing in clinical practice*. Washington, DC and London: American Psychiatric Publishing.

Armstrong, D. (2006a). Emotions in organizations: Disturbance or intelligence. In R. French (Ed.), *Organization in the mind* (pp. 90–110). London: Karnac.

Armstrong, D. (2006b). The analytic object in organizational work. In R. French (Ed.), *Organization in the mind* (pp. 44–55). London: Karnac.

Ballin Klein, D. (1977). *The unconscious: Invention or discovery*. Santa Monica, CA: Goodyear Publishing.

Balthzard, P. A., Cooke, R. A., & Potter, R. E. (2006). Dysfunctional culture, dysfunctional organization: Capturing the behavioral norms that form organizational culture and drive performance. *Journal of Managerial Psychology, 21*(8), 709–732.

Banet, A. G., Jr., & Hayden, C. (1977). The Tavistock primer. In J. E. Jones & J. W. Pfeiffer (Eds.), *The 1977 annual handbook for group facilitators*. San Diego, CA: University Associates.

Bargh, J. A. (2014). Our unconscious mind. *Scientific American, 1*, 30–37.

Bartholomew, K., & Horowitz, L. M. (1991). Attachment styles among young adults. A test of a four-category model. *Journal of Personality and Social Psychology, 61*, 226–244.

Bass, B. M. (1990). From transactional to transformational leadership: Learning to share the vision. *Organizational Dynamics, 18*(3), 19–31.

Beck, U. C. (2012). *Psychodynamic coaching: Focus and depth*. London: Karnac.

Bettelheim, B., & Karlin, D. (1983). *Liebe als Therapie. Gespräche über das Seelenleben des Kindes*. Zürich: Piper.

Bingham, C. B., & Eisenhardt, K. M. (2011). Rational heuristics. The 'Simple Rules' that strategists learn from process experience. *Strategic Management Journal, 32*/3, 1437–1464.

Bion, W. R. (1961). *Experiences in groups and other papers.* New York: Basic Books.

Bion, W. R. (1962). *Learning from experience.* London: Karnac.

Bion, W. R. (1970). *Attention and interpretation: A scientific approach to insights in psychoanalysis.* London: Tavistock.

Bostrom, N. (2014). *Superintelligence: Paths, dangers, strategies.* Oxford: Oxford University Press.

Bowlby, J. (1969). *Attachment and loss. Volume 1: Attachment.* London: Hogarth Press.

Bowlby, J. (1973). *Attachment and loss. Volume 2: Separation, Anxiety and Anger.* London: Hogarth Press.

Bowlby, J. (1980). *Attachment and loss. Volume 3: Loss, Sadness and Depression.* London: Hogarth Press.

Bowlby, J. (1988). *Parent-child attachment and healthy human development.* London: Routledge.

Brennan, D., & Wildflower, L. (2014). Ethics in coaching. In E. Cox, T. Bachkirova, & D. Clutterbuck (Eds.), *The complete handbook of coaching* (2nd ed., pp. 430–444). London: Sage.

Brown, A. D., & Starkey, K. (2000). Organizational identity and learning: A psychodynamic perspective. *Academy of Management Review, 25*(1), 101–120.

Brunning, H. (2006). The six domains of executive coaching. In H. Brunning (Ed.), *Executive coaching: Systems-psychodynamic perspective* (pp. 131–151). London: Karnac.

Brynjolfsson, E., & MacAfee, A. (2014). *The second machine age: Work, progress, and prosperity in a time of brilliant technologies.* New York: W W Norton & Co.

Buckley, W. (1967). *Sociology and modern system theory.* Englewood Cliffs, NJ: Prentice Hall.

Campbell, J. P. (1983). Some possible implications of "modelling" for the conceptualization of measurement. In F. Lamdy, S. Zedeck, & J. Cleveland (Eds.), *Performance measurement and theory* (pp. 277–298). Hillsdale, NJ: Lawrence Erlbaum Associates Inc.

Carver, C. S., & Schreier, M. F. (1992). *Perspectives on personality* (2nd ed.). Needham Heughts, MA: Allyn and Bacon.

Chapman, J. (2006). Anxiety and defective decision making: An elaboration of the groupthink model in management decision. *Management Decision, 44*(10), 1391–1404.

Clutterbuck, D. (2014). Team coaching. In E. Cox, T. Bachkirova, & D. Clutterbuck (Eds.), *The complete handbook of coaching* (2nd ed., pp. 271–284). London: Sage.

Cyert, R. M. M., & March, J. G. (1963). *A behavioral theory of the firm*. Englewood Cliffs, NJ: Prentice Hall.

Damasio, A. R. (1999). *The feeling of what happens: Body and emotion in the making of consciousness*. New York, NY: Harcourt Brace.

Damasio, A. R. (2010). *Self comes to mind: Constructing the conscious brain*. New York, NY: Pantheon/Random House.

Day, A. (2010). Coaching at relational depth: A case study. *Journal of Management Development, 29*(10), 864–876.

Dennett, D. (2017). *From Bacteria to Bach and back. The evolution of mind*. New York, NY and London: W.W. Norton & Company.

Diverseo SAS. (2012). *The unconscious sealing*. Women in Leadership.

Eden, A. (2006). Coaching women for senior executive roles: A societal perspective on power and exclusion. In H. Brunning (Ed.), *Executive coaching. Systems-psychodynamic perspective* (pp. 79–94). London: Karnac.

Eisold, K. (2005). Using Bion. *Psychoanalytic Psychology, 22*, 357–369.

Ellenberger, H. F. (1970). *The discovery of the unconscious: The history and evolution of dynamic psychiatry*. New York, NY: Basic Books.

Elliotts, J. (1955). Social systems as a defence against persecutory and depressive anxiety. In M. Klein, P. Heimann, & R. Morey-Kyrle (Eds.), *New directions in psychoanalysis* (pp. 478–498). London: Tavistock Publications.

Ettin, M. F., Cohen, B. D., & Fidler, J. W. (1997). Group-as-a-whole theory viewed in its 20th-century context. *Group Dynamics: Theory, Research, and Practice, 1*(4), 329–340.

Fonagy, P., Gergely, G., Jurist, E., & Target, M. (2002). *Affect regulation, mentalization and the development of the self*. New York, NY: Other Press.

Fotopoulou A (2012). Towards psychodynamic neuroscience. In A. Fotopoulou, M. Conway, & D. Pfaff (Eds.), *From the couch to the lab: Trends in psychodynamic neuroscience* (pp. 25–48). Oxford: Oxford University Press.

French, R., & Simpson, P. (2010). The "work group": Redressing the balance in Bion's experience in groups. *Human relations, 63*(12), 1859–1878.

Freud, A. (1936/2003). *Das Ich und die Abwehrmechanismen* (18th ed.). Frankfurt am Main: Fischer.

Freud, S. (1901). *Gesammelte Werke: IV: Zur Psychopathologie des Alltagslebens*. London: Imago Publishing Co., Ltd.

Freud, S. (1905). *Gesammelte Werke: V: Psychische Behandlung (Seelenbehandlung)* (pp. 287–315). Frankfurt am Main: Fischer.

Freud, S. (1912a). *Gesammelte Werke: VIII: Einige Bemerkungen über den Begriff des Unbewussten in der Psychoanalyse* (pp. 430–439). Frankfurt am Main: Fischer.

Freud, S. (1912b). *Gesammelte Werke: VIII: Zur Dynamik der Übertragung.* Frankfurt am Main: Fischer.

Freud, S. (1923). *Gesammelte Werke: XIII: Das Ich und das Es* (pp. 236–289). Frankfurt am Main: Fischer.

Fromm, E. (1947). *Man for himself: An inquiry into the psychology of ethic.* London: Routledge.

Gal, D., & Rucker, D. (2017, September 30). The loss of loss aversion: Will it loom larger than its gain? *Journal of Consumer Psychology,* Forthcoming. Retrieved from SSRN: https://ssrn.com/abstract=3049660

Gigerenzer, G. (2007). *Gut feelings: The intelligence of the unconscious.* New York, NY: Penguin.

Gigerenzer, G., Todd, P., & ABC Group. (2001). *Simple heuristics that make us smart.* Oxford: Oxford University Press.

Gilbert, D. T. (2006). *Stumbling on happiness.* New York: Random House.

Goleman, D. (1995). *Emotional intelligence: Why it can matter more than IQ.* New York, NY: Bantam Book.

Goleman, D., & Boyatzis, R. E. (2017). Emotional intelligence has 12 elements. Which do you need to work on? *Harvard Business Review, 17*(6).

Gould, L., Stapley, L., & Stein, M. (2001). *Systems psychodynamics of organizations* (p. 2ff). New York: Karnac.

Günter, G. (1999). *Traditionslinien des „Unbewussten". Schopenhauer – Nietzsche – Freud.* Tübingen: Edition Diskord.

Hadamard, J. S. (1945). *A Mathematician's mind: Testimonial for an essay on the psychology of invention in the mathematical field.* Princeton, NJ: Princeton University Press.

Hartley, C. A., & Phelps, E. A. (2012). Anxiety and decision-making. *Biological Psychiatry, 72*(2), 113–118.

Hartmann, E. (1869/2017). *Philosophy des Unbewussten.* Berlin: Contumax.

Hirschhorn, L. (1999). The primary risk. *Human Relations, 52*(1), 5–23.

Holzkamp-Osterkamp, U. (1975). *Grundlagen der Motivationsforschung.* Frankfurt am Main and New York, NY: Campus.

Huffington, C. (2006). A contextualized approach to coaching. In H. Brunning (Ed.), *Executive coaching: Systems-psychodynamic perspective* (pp. 41–78). London: Karnac.

Hüther, G. (2005). *Biologie der Angst: Wie aus Stress Gefühle werden.* Göttingen: Vandenhoeck und Ruprecht.

Jacobi, J. (1957). *Komplex, archetypus, symbol in der Psychologie C.G. Jungs.* Zürich and Stuttgart: Rascher.

Janis, J. (1972). *Victims of groupthink: A psychological study of foreign-policy decisions and fiascoes.* Boston, MA: Houghton Mifflin.

Jung, C. G. (1916). The psychology of dreams. In C. E. Long (Ed.), *Collected papers on analytical psychology.* London: Baillière, Tindall and Cox.

Jung, C. G. (1935). Allgemeine probleme der psychotherapie (General problems of psychotherapy CW16). *Zentralblatt für Psychotherapie, VIII*(2), 66–82.

Jung, C. G. (1946). *Die Psychologie der Übertragung (The psychology of transference)*. Zürich: Rascher.

Jung, C. G. (1959). Die transzendente Funktion. In C. G. Jung (Ed.), *Gesammelte Werke, Die Dynamik des Unbewussten* (Vol. 8, pp. 85–108). Solothurn and Düsseldorf: Walter.

Jung, C. G. (1964). Zugang zum Unbewussten. In C. G. Jung (Ed.), *Der Mensch und seine Symbole* (16th ed., pp. 18–103). Ostfildern: Patmos Verlag (Approach to the unconscious in: Man and his symbols).

Katz, D., & Kahn, R. L. (1966). *The social psychology of organisations*. New York, NY: Wiley.

Keats, J. (1970). *The letters of John Keats: A selection* (R. Gittings, Ed.). Oxford: Oxford University Press.

Kernberg, O. F. (1984). *Severe personality disorders: Psychotherapeutic strategies*. New Haven, CT: Yale University.

Kernberg, O. F. (1998). Regression in organizational leadership. In M. Kets de Vries (Ed.), *The irrational executive: Psychoanalytic studies in management*. New York: International Universities Press.

Kernberg, O. F. (2006). *Schwere Persönlichkeitsstörungen*. Stuttgart: Klett-Cotta.

Kernberg, O. F., & Caligor, E. (2005). A psychoanalytic theory of personality disorders. In M. F. Lenzenweger & J. F. Clarkin (Eds.), *Major theories of personality disorder* (2nd ed., pp. 114–156). New York, NY and London: Gilford Press.

Kets de Vries, M. (2004). Organizations on the couch: A clinical perspective on organizational dynamics. *European Management Journal, 22*(2), 183–200.

Kets de Vries, M. F. R. (2006). *The leader on the couch: A clinical approach to changing people and organizations*. San Francisco, CA: Jossey-Bass.

Kets de Vries, M. F. R. (2011). *The hedgehog effect: The secrets of building high performance teams*. San Francisco, CA: Jossey Bass.

Kets de Vries, M. F. R., & Miller, D. (1984). *The neurotic organization*. San Francisco, CA: Jossey-Bass.

Kets De Vries, M. F. R., & Engellau, E. (2010). A clinical approach to the dynamics of leadership and executive transformation. In N. Nohria & R. Khurana (Eds.), *Handbook of leadership theory and practice* (pp. 183–222). Boston, MA: Harvard University Press.

Kets de Vries, M. F. R., & Miller, D. (1997). Narcissism and leadership: An object relations perspective. In R. P. Vecchio (Ed.), *Leadership: Understanding the dynamics of power and influence in organizations* (pp. 194–214). Notre Dame, IN: University of Notre Dame Press.

Kihlstrom, J. F. (2013). Unconscious processes. In D. Reisberg (Ed.), *Oxford library of psychology. The Oxford handbook of cognitive psychology* (pp. 176–186). New York, NY: Oxford University Press.

Kihlstrom, J. F., Tobias, B. A., Mulvaney, S., & Tobis, I. P. (2000). The emotional unconscious. In E. Eich, J. F. Kihlstrom, G. H. Bower, J. P. Forgas, & P. M. Niedenthal (Eds.), *Counterpoints: Cognition and emotion* (pp. 30–86). New York, NY: Oxford University Press.

Kinzel, C. (2002) *Arbeit und Psyche. Konzepte und Perspektiven einer psychodynamischen Organisationstheorie.* Stuttgart: Kohlhammer.

Kilburg, R. (2004). When shadows fall: Using psychodynamic approaches in executive coaching. *Consulting Psychology Journal: Practice and Research, 56*(4), 246–268.

Kimbles, S. L., & Singer, T. (2004). *The cultural complex: Contemporary Jungian perspectives on psyche and society*. London: Brunner-Routledge.

Kohut, H. (1966). Forms and transformations of narcissism. *Journal of the American Psychoanalytic Association, 14*(2), 243–272.

Kurzweil, R. (2006). *The singularity is near: When humans transcend biology*. London: Penguin.

Kwiatkowski, R. (2006). Inside-out and outside-in: The use of personality and 360 degree data in executive coaching. In H. Brunning (Ed.), *Executive coaching: Systems-psychodynamic perspective* (pp. 153–182). London: Karnac.

Laplanche, J., & Pontalis, J. B. (1972). *Das Vokabular der Psychoanalyse*. Frankfurt am Main: Suhrkamp.

Lawrence, G. (2006). Executive coaching, unconscious thinking, and infinity. In H. Brunning (Ed.), *Executive coaching: Systems-psychodynamic perspective* (pp. 97–112). London: Karnac.

LeDoux, J. (1998). *The emotional brain*. London: Weidenfels and Nicolson.

Lee, G. (2014). The psychodynamic approach to coaching. In E. Cox, T. Bachkirova, & D. Clutterbuck (Eds.), *The complete handbook of coaching* (2nd ed., pp. 21–34). London: Sage.

Lencioni, P. (2002). *The five dysfunctions of a team*. San Francisco, CA: Jossey Bass.

Leuzinger-Bohleber, M., Stuhr, U., Rüger, B., & Beutel, M. (2003). How to study the "quality of psychoanalytic treatments" and their long-term effects on patients' well-being: A representative, multi-perspective follow-up study. *International Journal of Psychoanalysis, 84*, 263–290.

Lévi-Strauss, C. (1958/1949). L'éfficacité symbolique. In C. Lévi-Strauss (Ed.), *Anthropologie structurale* (pp. 220–225). Paris: Plon (English translation: "The Effectiveness of Symbols", in *Structural anthropology*, pp. 186–205, trans. C. Jacobson & B. Grundfest Schoepf, New York: Basic Books, 1963.) (Orig. pub 1949).

Lier, D. (2009, Fall). Symbolic life. *Spring: A Journal of Archetype and Culture*, *82*.

Lipps, T. (1896/1989). Der Begriff des Unbewussten in der Psychologie. In L. Lütkehaus (Ed.), *Das wahre innere Afrika: Texte zur Entdeckung des Unbewussten vor Freud* (pp. 235–252). Giessen: Psychosozialverlag.

Long, S. (2016). The transforming experience framework. In S. Long (Ed.), *Transforming experience in organisations: A framework for organisational research and consultancy* (pp. 1–15). London: Karnac.

Lütkehaus, L. (2005). Einleitung. In L. Lütkehaus (Ed.), *Das wahre innere Afrika: Texte zur Entdeckung des Unbewussten vor Freud* (pp. 7–45). Giessen: Psychosozialverlag.

Maccoby, M. (2000, January/February). Narcissistic leaders: The incredible pros, the inevitable cons. *Harvard Business Review*.

Maccoby, M. (2004). *The productive narcissist: The promise and peril of visionary leadership*. New York, NY: Broadway Books.

MacIntyre, A. C. (1958). *The unconscious: A conceptual study*. London: Routledge.

March, J. G., & Simon, H. (1958). *Organisations*. New York, NY: Wiley.

Massey, I. (1990). Freud before Freud. In K. A. Scherner (Ed.), *The Centennial Review*, *34*(4), 567–576.

Mc Neill, B., & Worthen, V. (1989). The parallel process in psychotherapeutic supervision. *Professional Psychology: Research and Practice*, *20*(5), 329–333.

Mentzos, S. (2009). *Lehrbuch der Psychodynamik. Die Funktion der Dysfunktionalität psychischer Störungen*. Göttingen: Vandenhoeck und Ruprecht.

Messer, S. B. (2002). A psychodynamic perspective on resistance in psychotherapy: Vive la résistance. *Journal of Clinical Psychology*, *58*(2), 157–163.

Miller, E. J., & Rice, A. K. (1967). *Systems of organization: The control of task and sentient boundaries*. London: Tavistock.

Motowildo, S. S., Borman, W. C., & Schmitt, M. J. (1997). A theory of individual difference in task and contextual performance. *Human Performance*, *10*(2), 71–83.

Müller, L., & Knoll, D. (1998). *Ins Innere der Dinge schauen*. Düsseldorf: Patmos/Walter.

Nagel, C. (2014). *Behavioral strategy: Thoughts and feelings in the decision-making process. The unconscious and corporate success*. Bonn: Unternehmermedien.

Nagel, C. (2017). Behavioural strategy and deep foundations of dynamic capabilities. Using psychodynamic concepts to better deal with uncertainty in strategic management. *Global Economics and Management Review*, *21*(1–2), 46–64.

Nagel, T. (1974). What is it like to be a bat? *The Philosophical Review*, *83*(4), 435–450.

Newton, J., Long, S., & Sievers, B. (Eds.). (2006). *Coaching in depth: The organizational role analysis approach*. London: Karnac.

Nicholls, A., & Liebscher, M. (Eds.). (2010). *Thinking the unconscious: Nineteenth-century German thought*. Cambridge: Cambridge University Press.

Oberholser, J. C. (1993). Elements of the Socratic method: I. Systematic questioning. *Psychotherapy*, *30*(1), 67–74.

Obholzer, A. (2006). Foreword. In H. Brunning (Ed.), *Executive coaching: Systems-psychodynamic perspective* (pp. XI–XXIV). London: Karnac.

Odgen, T. H. (1979). On projective identification. *International Journal of Psychoanalysis*, *60*, 357–373.

Otabe, T. (2013). Das Unbewusste im letzten Viertel des 18. Jhds aus ästhtischer Sicht. *Journal of the Faculty of Letters, The University of Tokyo, Aesthetics*, *38*, 59–70.

Panksepp, J. (1998). *Affective neuroscience: The foundations of human and animal emotions*. Oxford: Oxford University Press.

Panksepp, J., & Biven, L. (2012). *The archeology of mind: Neuroevolutionary origins of human emotions*. New York, NY and London: W.W. Norton & Company.

Peltier, B. (2010). *The psychology of executive coaching: Theory and application* (2nd ed.). New York, NY: Routledge.

Peters, O., & Gell-Mann, M. (2016). Evaluating gambles using dynamics. *Chaos*, *26*, 023103. https://doi.org/10.1063/1.4940236

Pohl, S. (1999). Unbewusste. In P. Prechtl & F. P. Burkhard (Eds.), *Metzlers Philosophielexikon* (2nd ed., pp. 615–616). Stuttgart and Weimar: J.B. Metzler.

Pooley, J. (2006). Layers of meaning: A coaching journey. In H. Brunning (Ed.), *Executive coaching: Systems-psychodynamic perspective* (pp. 113–130). London: Karnac.

Rauen, C. (2008). *Coaching*. Göttingen, Bern, Wien, Paris, Oxford and Prag: Hogrefe.

Reed, B., & Bazalgette, J. (2006). Organisational role analysis at the Grubb Institute of Behavioral Studies: Origins and developments. In J. Newton, S. Long, & B. Sievers (Eds.), *Coaching in depth: The organizational role analysis approach* (pp. 43–62). London: Karnac.

Riemann, F. (1961). *Grundformen der Angst*. München: Reinhardt.

Roberts, V. Z., & Jarrett, M. (2006). What is the difference and what makes the difference? A comparative study of psychodynamic and non-psychodynamic approaches to executive coaching. In H. Brunning (Ed.), *Executive coaching: Systems-psychodynamic perspective* (pp. 3–39). London: Karnac.

Rohde-Dachser, C. (2005, November 5). Konzepte des Unbewussten. *Festvortrag zum 40-jährigen Bestehen des Lehrinstituts*. http://www.psa-werkstattberichte.de/Originalarbeiten/originalarbeiten.html

Rose, J. D. (2011). Diverse perspectives on the Groupthink theory – A literary review. *Emerging Leadership Journeys*, 4(1), 37–57.

Rosenthal, S. (2006). Narcissism and leadership: A review and research agenda. *Working Paper: Centre for Public Leadership*, Harvard University.

Roth, G., & Ryba, A. (2016). *Coaching, Beratung und Gehirn*. Stuttgart: Klett-Cotta.

Roth, W. (2003). *Einführung in die Psychologie C.G. Jungs*. Düsseldorf and Zürich: Walter.

Sandler, C. (2011). *Executive coaching: A psychodynamic approach*. Berkshire: Open University Press.

Schad, J., Lewis M., Raisch, S., & Smith, W. K. (2016). Paradox research in management science: Looking back to move forward. *The Academy of Management Annals*, 10(1), 5–64.

Schreyögg, A. (2010). *Supervision. Ein Lehrbuch*. (5. erw. ed.). Wiesbaden: Verlag für Sozialwissenschaften.

Schruijer, S., & Vansina, L. (2008). Working across organisational boundaries: Understanding and working with intergroup dynamics. In L. Vansina & M.-J. Vansina-Cobbaert (Eds.), *Psychodynamics for consultants and managers* (pp. 390–412). Chichester: Wiley-Blackwell.

Searles, H. F. (1955). The informational value of supervisor's emotional experience. *Psychiatry*, 18, 135–146.

Sievers, B., & Beumer, U. (2006). Organizational role analysis and consultation. The organization as inner object. In J. Newton, S. Long, & B. Sievers (Eds.), *Coaching in depth: The organizational role analysis approach* (pp. 65–81). London: Karnac.

Simon, H. A. (1947). *Administrative behavior*. New York, NY: MacMillan.

Simon, H. A. (1957). *Models of man*. New York, NY: Wiley.

Simpson, P., & French, R. (2006). Negative capability and the capacity to think in the present moment: Some implications for leadership practice. *Leadership*, 2(2), 245–255.

Simpson, P., French, R., & Harvey, C. (2002). Leadership and negative capability. *Human Relations*, 55(10), 1209–1226.

Singer, T., & Lamm, C. (2009). The social neuroscience of empathy. In The year in cognitive neuroscience 2009. *Annals of the New York Academy of Sciences*, 1156, 81–96

Solms, M. (2013). The conscious ID. *Neuropsychoanalysis*, 15(1), 5–19.

Solms, M. (2014). A neuropsychoanalytical approach to the hard problem of consciousness. *Journal of Integrative Neuroscience*, 13(2), 173–185.

Solms, M. (2015). Depression, A neurpsychoanalytic perspective. In M. Solms (Ed.), *The feeling brain: Selected papers on neuropsychoanalysis* (pp. 95–108). London: Karnac.

Solms, M. (2017). A practical introduction to neuropsychoanalysis: Clinical implications. *NPSA Workshop*, Frankfurt am Main, 27–28 May 2017.

Spero, M. (2006). Coaching as a transitional process: A case of a lawyer in transition. In H. Brunning (Ed.), *Executive coaching: Systems-psychodynamic perspective* (pp. 217–235). London: Karnac.

Stavemann, H. H. (2002). *Sokratische Gesprächsführung in Therapie und Beratung*. Weinheim and Basel: Beltz.

Taleb, N. N. (2018). *Skin in the game*. New York, NY: Random House.

Teece, D. J. (2007). Explicating dynamic capabilities: The nature and microfoundations of (sustainable) enterprise performance. *Strategic Management Journal, 28*, 1319–1350.

Triest, J. (1999). The inner drama of role taking in organizations. In R. French & R. Vince (Eds.), *Group relations, management, and organization* (pp. 209–223). Oxford: Oxford University Press.

Valerio, A. M. (2009). *Developing women leaders: A guide for men and women in organisations*. Chichester: Wiley.

Vansina, L. (2008). Psychodynamics: A field for study and an approach. In L. Vansina & M.-J. Vansina-Cobbaert (Eds.), *Psychodynamics for consultants and managers* (pp. 108–155). New York: Wiley-Blackwell.

Völmicke, E. (2005). *Das Unbewusste im Deutschen Idealismus*. Würzburg: Könighausen & Neumann.

Whyte, L. L. (1978). *The unconscious before Freud*. London, Dover: F. Pinter.

Winnicott, D. (1960). The theory of the parent-infant relationship. *International Journal of Psycho-Analysis, 41*, 585–595.

Wulf, C. (2005). Präsenz und Absenz. Prozess und Struktur in der Seele. In G. Jüttemann, M. Sonntag, & C. Wulf (Eds.), *Die Seele. Ihre Geschichte im Abendland*. Göttingen: Vandenhoek & Ruprecht.

Yechiam, E. (2018). Acceptable losses: The debatable origins of loss aversion. *Psychological Research*. https://doi.org/10.1007/s00426-018-1013-8

Index

Note: numbers in **bold** indicate tables and numbers in *italics* indicate figures on the corresponding pages.